'Who knew there were so many uses for marmalade. ... guides you through all kinds of savoury and sweet ideas, from sticky buns to bacon sandwiches.' *Red*

'Sarah Randell's cookbook offers endless recipe suggestions for the preserve.' *Daily Telegraph*

'Once you have tried making homemade marmalade, you will never turn back.' *The Foodie Bugle blog*

'Essential reading.' *Evening Standard*

'Perfect for any foodies out there.' *Grazia*

'Fabulous recipes.' *Saga Magazine*

'Sarah Randell's book provides an amnesty for all those who love to make marmalade and then use it up.'
Rose Prince, *Daily Telegraph*

'Indulge your inner Paddington Bear.' *Homes and Gardens*

'Sarah Randell has written some lip-smacking recipes for marmalade and what you can do with it.' *Herald*

'If you've ever wondered how Paddington likes his marmalade sandwiches, now you can find out.' *Guardian*

Sarah Randell is a food writer and editor and was Food Director at *Sainsbury's Magazine* for over ten years. She previously worked as food editor for Delia Smith's cookery books and on many of Delia's BBC TV programmes. Sarah lives in London with her husband and little boy Archie.

Follow her on Twitter: @2015bittersweet

www.potofmarmalade.uk

A POT OF
MARMALADE

THE ULTIMATE GUIDE TO MAKING
AND COOKING WITH MARMALADE

SARAH RANDELL
Foreword by José Pizarro

SALT · YARD
BOOK Cº

First published as *Marmalade: A Bittersweet Cookbook* in Great Britain in 2014
by Saltyard Books.
An imprint of Hodder & Stoughton
An Hachette UK Company

First published in paperback in 2016

I

Sarah Randell © 2014

A CIP catalogue record for this title is available from the British Library

ISBN 978 1 444 78431 2

Typeset in Gill Sans by Palimpsest Book Production Limited, Falkirk, Stirlingshire

Printed and bound by Clays Ltd, St Ives plc

John Murray policy is to use papers that are natural, renewable and recyclable
products and made from wood grown in sustainable forests. The logging and
manufacturing
regulations of t

Saltyard books
Carmelite Hou
50 Victoria Emi
London EC4Y

www.saltyardb

CONTENTS

BREAKFAST & BRUNCH   73

LUNCH & SUPPER 95

PUDDINGS 125

TEATIME 167

DRINKS & COCKTAILS   197

ACKNOWLEDGEMENTS   213

INDEX   215

FOREWORD
BY JOSÉ PIZARRO

Sarah is right when she tells us that the Spanish, in general, do not value the bitter orange or a pot of marmalade. As she knows, I am the exception. I adore marmalade. So, when I was given the opportunity to write this foreword, I was both honoured and delighted. Growing up in Spain, I thought marmalade was something only the English ate. Then I moved to England and I ate it too. Lots of it, usually accompanied by a cup of tea. Being keen cooks, I don't think it is in our Spanish genes to ignore the Seville orange and marmalade, and doing so just seems to have become a very bad habit.

When I go back home I fly into Sevilla. At Easter time, when the bitter orange trees are flowering, you can almost get high on the heady scent of the *azahar*, the pretty white orange blossom. It's something that is very special to me, and Sarah's evocative writing transports me from the grey concrete of London, where I now live, to the Barrio Santa Cruz in springtime, the warm air richly perfumed with the scent of orange.

For most people, marmalade is just for breakfast time. Nothing wrong with that, especially if you take the time to make it yourself. I can't wait to make some of the tempting marmalades in this book; lemon and gin marmalade, which combines two of my favourite ingredients, is top of my 'must make' list. Once you have made your own marmalade, you will probably never bother to buy a jar again, and a pot of marmalade is such a perfect gift – there's a lifetime of presents in this book! But it isn't just about

memorable marmalades: Sarah has shown us how to use marmalade to make exciting meals for any time of the day. The flavours
and contrasts are exciting and inspired, and some of the recipes
are genius – what about toast and marmalade tart? I love it!

That Sarah has produced a wonderful book which is a solid
reference as well as a source of inspiration is no surprise to me;
her depth of knowledge and enthusiasm for food are rare. Sarah
understands the home cook better than most, as is reflected in
this recipe treasury – it promises great things and I can't wait to
get cooking.

José Pizarro
March 2014

INTRODUCTION

There is something irresistibly cosy about marmalade. Thickly spread on generously buttered bread or toast, all you need to complete the moment is a cup of tea and suddenly everything feels all right with the world. Marmalade on toast is as comforting as eggs with soldiers or scones topped with clotted cream and strawberry jam. Certain foods are meant for each other: toast, melting butter and a burst of tangy fruit with a hint of bitterness is a marriage made in heaven.

Some people stand by the bitterness of marmalade as the perfect chaser to fried eggs and bacon, but in my childhood, although we ate plenty of good food, a cooked breakfast wasn't held in great reverence. I'm still not a fan. Bacon sandwiches aside, I'm a sweet-toothed girl in the morning. Toast and preserve were the anchor of our family morning table; there was always a pot of good marmalade to dig into and set our tastebuds jingling. Toast and marmalade seems to me to be emblematic of a British way of life and is firmly buried in our culinary psyche, as well as being one of our culinary ambassadors around the world.

A few years ago, I was asked if I would become a judge at the World's Original Marmalade Awards. One bitterly cold February morning, I found myself at the door of the grand stately home of Dalemain in Cumbria, home to the awards and to the originator of the marmalade festival, Jane Hasell-McCosh. Boxes and boxes of jars of competitors' marmalade had been arriving for weeks and there were row upon row of trestle tables laden with jars.

I spent two days blind-tasting with fellow judges, following strict criteria and eating a lot of marmalade, and I mean a lot. Some were irresistible, some were pretty awful, but the thing that fascinated me was that every pot of the several hundred in the room was different.

Marmalade is a humble preserve. You need only a few ingredients to have a go at making your own – citrus fruit (the defining ingredient), sugar, water and maybe a spice or two or a dash of alcohol – and the variations are endless. Seville oranges, the heart of a classic marmalade, are harvested in Andalucía from the beginning of December, but the larger English suppliers tend to wait until the frenetic shopping sprees of Christmas are past before they stock up. Introduced to Europe from Asia, these knobbly-skinned citrus fruits have a short season, usually around six weeks. Once, the oranges arrived from Spain by rail, but today they are shipped. They are a burst of vibrant colour and a reminder of Mediterranean sunshine when there is little other fruit around to play with in the kitchen. And then they vanish. Just like that – impossible to find until the following winter. Very few other fruits are so true to their season.

Seville oranges may not be the glamour models of the citrus family but they pack a punch in flavour with their sweet perfume and bitter edge that provides the perfect foil for sugar, the preserver.

On a winter's day, hunkering down to create a pot of marmalade is very satisfying; the warmth of the kitchen, the scent of citrus that pervades the house and the steam settling as it hits the icy windows are, for me, all part of the joy. Marmalade-making is no quick fix; I usually set aside half a day and look forward to the ritual. I'm all for fast, vibrant cooking on busy days but sometimes it's a relief to slow down; making marmalade is one of the most enjoyable slow-food experiences. The line of jars filled to the brim with golden goodness can't help but induce a warm, slightly smug, glow from within.

We love to share marmalade recipes that are family favourites, embedded in local tradition or just personally special to us. The pride in transforming a group of simple raw ingredients into something so special that you can store and share with others or give as a present that, in turn, rewards us with nostalgic, frugal satisfaction.

If you haven't ever made a pot of preserve, let me convince you to join the marmalade movement. With a few basic instructions, it really is simple. You don't need lots of kit and you will soon discover favourite fruit combinations and experiment with your own variations and recipes. Homemade marmalade isn't just for the breakfast table; it adds a special something to a lot of recipes.

A POTTED HISTORY

WHERE DID MARMALADE BEGIN?

Not in England and not with oranges. The Greeks, followed by the
Romans, slowly cooked quince with honey to sweeten it. The
Greek quince preserve was called *melomeli* (apple in honey). It
was a way of making something edible out of an otherwise very
stubborn fruit, and the pectin – then, a mysterious ingredient –
enabled the fruit pastes to set.

The name marmalade has developed from the Portuguese word
marmelada, referring to quince paste, made from *marmelo*, or
quince. It is thought that the Moors first introduced *marmelada* to
the Portuguese, and in Tudor times boxes of quince paste (similar
to *membrillo*) from Portugal arrived at the ports of Britain. It was
eaten in the homes of royalty and wealthy English families as a
sweetmeat, often given as an exquisite gift. English recipes using
quince also existed (often called *chardequince*), and spices and
flavourings, such as cinnamon, ginger, rose water and musk, were
used in these homemade thick preserves. They were set in
moulds, and served at the end of lavish banquets in the sixteenth
and seventeenth centuries to aid digestion; they were even
considered an aphrodisiac.

From the seventeenth century sugar was more readily available
and affordable and marmalades made from other fruits became
more common and, by the early eighteenth century, English family
recipes for softer-set citrus marmalade using imported bitter

oranges and sugar developed, some with shredded peel. Marmalade was no longer eaten only as an expensive sweetmeat or added to desserts, but became a preserve to be enjoyed in its own right – a staple at the British breakfast table. In other parts of Europe, marmalade was, and still is, used as a more generic term for all types of preserve and jam – Spanish *marmelada*, Italian *marmellata* or French *marmelade*. In Britain, we are purists; our marmalade is made from citrus fruit and, usually, has shredded peel suspended in the jelly.

THE MARMALADE WE KNOW TODAY

It was the Keiller family who first made shredded marmalade commercially. James Keiller was a grocer in Dundee, and in the eighteenth century, so the story goes, he bought a batch of Seville oranges from a Spanish ship that was taking refuge from harsh storms. Realising they couldn't sell the bitter oranges for the fruit bowl, James and his wife experimented, cooking them with sugar, using supplies from his grocery business. So popular was the preserve they made that Keiller marmalade, packaged in white glass jars, was subsequently sold in the family shop. To meet with demand, they opened a factory in 1797 and other Scottish manufacturers copied the trend. Today there is a plethora of well-known marmalade brands, but homemade seems to be more popular than ever.

A TRIP TO SOUTHERN SPAIN

As with grapes grown for making specific wines, I wondered if the terroir of Seville, in the south of Spain, was essential for imparting fine flavour to bitter oranges. Wilkin & Sons have been making top-quality marmalade (and other preserves) at Tiptree in Essex since 1885, following encouragement by prime minister William Gladstone to make 'money from jam'. Wilkin's only use Seville oranges in their marmalade. 'We've tried fruit from other areas of the world,' Peter Wilkin explained, 'but they don't have the same flavour. You can't make a silk purse out of a sow's ear. It has to be the Seville oranges for marmalade, they are unique.' So, to Seville I went.

The Arabs dominated Seville from as early as 712 and introduced the first bitter oranges (and lemons) to the Mediterranean; orange groves were soon established in this sunny corner of Spain. Bitter oranges and Seville are now so intertwined that the names are inextricably linked, marmalade-makers often referring to marmalade oranges simply as Sevilles.

The streets of Seville are lined with bitter orange trees and in the spring the heady scent of the orange blossom, or *azahar*, is intoxicating. Yet, despite the many trees and their expertise in growing the bitter orange, the Spanish don't actually eat them. All the oranges are exported – in fact, it's a challenge to find a bitter orange at the food market in Seville. 'Unless locals have their own trees, they don't cook with bitter oranges,' Seville-based chef Willy Moya declared, 'and even then it would be unusual to make

---

marmalade. Marmalade isn't part of the food culture of Seville – the bitter orange farms exist because of the English.'

There is one group of keen cooks in Seville who have a long tradition of making marmalades: the Andalucían nuns. I found my way through the winding streets of Seville to the Monastery of Santa Paula. I tentatively rang the bell and waited in front of the dark heavy door, which gave nothing away. A beaming Sister beckoned me inside, and after much ham-handed sign language and her smiling, I managed to explain my mission and she brought out jar upon jar of beautiful marmalade and orange blossom jelly – an experience to treasure.

Over recent years, the co-operative of smaller Andalucían bitter orange farms has been consolidated and there are now fewer, larger growers. Some large historic companies that I visited, such as Bordas, specialise in the preparation of peel, pulp, juice and whole fruit, which are exported frozen to British makers. Others, such as Ave María Farm, export their organic fruit in wooden crates; their fresh oranges are second to none. I visited the Huerta María farm on a warm December day; it's a third-generation family business where marmalade is key to everything they do. Row upon row of bitter orange trees waved in the gentle breeze as the fruit was carefully harvested and packed into traditional wooden crates for export within Europe, predominantly to Britain.

MAKING MARMALADE – THE KIT

WEIGHING SCALES AND MEASURING JUG

At a pinch, you could get away without a set of scales if you are making a basic Seville orange marmalade, as you can buy a weight of oranges and the weight of sugar is printed on the bags. You will, however, need a measuring jug for liquids – most digital scales have millilitre measures but I still prefer to use a large measuring jug, and I find it easier to pour liquid from a measuring jug into the pan than from a bowl.

SQUEEZER

I have a large and a small squeezer to use for different sizes of citrus fruit, and a wooden reamer, which I use for fruit that doesn't have pips, such as limes.

PRESERVING PAN

I had always used my mother's very large aluminium preserving pan until a recent investment in an all-singing-and-dancing stainless steel version, which is less cumbersome. It is also easy to clean – I soak it overnight and it takes minutes to wash the following day. It has a volume measure on the inside of the pan, which is useful, and a pouring lip, which is handy when you get to the end of potting up and you only have a little marmalade left in the bottom of the pan. If you are going to make marmalade every year I highly recommend buying one – you can also use it for jams and chutneys. Small batches of marmalade can be made in a large, deep, wide-based pan, but you need to watch carefully when the marmalade is at a rolling boil, as there is a risk it will bubble over the sides – dangerous, disheartening and no fun to clear up.

GAUZE OR MUSLIN

For most recipes, you will need squares of either of these materials to put the pips, pith and chopped peel on to – the material is then gathered up and tied to make a money-bag-shaped pouch, which is added to the pan when the fruit and liquid are simmering. I usually buy gauze from the chemist, simply because it is easier to find and cheaper than muslin; a 30 × 30cm double-layered square is usually about the right size and sturdy enough. Have a ball of kitchen string to hand too – if you don't have string, you can use a clean elastic band. I leave one end of the string long enough to be able to tie the pouch to the handle of the preserving pan and immerse it in the marmalade mix; this makes it easier to remove.

SPOONS

A long-handled wooden spoon is useful for stirring. You will also need a few cutlery spoons for testing the set of the marmalade. If you have a soup spoon, its deeper bowl makes it perfect for scooping out marmalade to test the set.

KITCHEN THERMOMETER

I own a kitchen thermometer, which clearly shows the setting temperature – 104.5°C. I sometimes use it to help me tell when my marmalade is near setting point, but I still find the wrinkle test the easiest method of all (see page 21).

SAUCERS

Make sure you have a few saucers to hand, ready to pop into the freezer so you can test for setting point using the wrinkle test.

MEASURING JUG OR LADLE

Both of these are useful for transferring the hot marmalade from the pan into the sterilised jars. I tend to use a small measuring jug, which I find easiest of all.

WIDE-NECKED FUNNEL

Not essential, but avoids messy filling of jars and is particularly
useful if you have jars with narrow necks.

JARS AND STERILISING

The fruit you use and the length of time you boil the marmalade
will affect the amount you make and the number of jars you need.
I have noted the volume made for each recipe as a guide – these
are based on a 340g jar for simplicity. Each 340g jar holds about
300ml.

If you are going to make marmalade in earnest, you will need
quite a collection of jars. The first port of call is friends and family;
ask them to save them for you and to make it their mission to eat
up the contents of jars with scant amounts remaining. Any jars will
do as long as they are not chipped, are clean and have tight-fitting
lids. If you have pre-used jars and the lids have corroded, throw
them out; you can use a waxed disc and a cellophane cover for
the jar instead or, even better, source a replacement lid.

You need to sterilise the jars (and the lids) before you use them.
First wash them in hot soapy water, then rinse them and place
them in the oven at 140°C/fan 120°C/gas 1 for 15–20 minutes.
Sterilise the lids at the same time, but first remove the rubber

---

bands from any clip-top jars. You need to fill the jars while they are hot – I sterilise them just before I bring my marmalade to a rolling boil to set it.

WAXED DISCS AND LABELS

Waxed discs create a seal on the top of the hot marmalade; make sure you put them into the jar wax (shiny) side down before securing a circular cellophane cover on top with an elastic band. Or, best of all, use a tight-fitting lid so that a waxed disc isn't necessary (although I do often still add it for nostalgic reasons as much as anything else). You can buy sets of waxed discs and cellophane covers from good cook-shops or online suppliers (see page 24). If you want to add patterned paper tops, put these over the lids once the jars are cold – I sometimes cut out circles from wrapping papers I particularly like or from simple brown parcel paper, and secure them with coloured string or ribbon. I prefer to use tie-on labels (see page 25), but adhesive labels are more practical if you are making a lot of marmalade. Stick them on the jars when the marmalade is cold – hot jars and sticky labels aren't a good mix, the labels will slide off.

MARMALADE BASICS

---

1. WHOLE FRUIT METHOD

The fruit is simmered whole, then shredded and further cooked with sugar.

---

2. JELLY METHOD

The fruit is juiced and shredded and the pith and pips are often put into a pouch to immerse in the cooking liquid when you simmer the peel in water and juice.

The whole fruit method is less time-consuming to prepare than the jelly method, but the jelly method will give a clearer result and I prefer it for elegant, fresh-tasting marmalades – this is the method I use for a classic Seville orange marmalade. The whole fruit method tends to give a fleshier, meatier end result. I vary the method depending on the fruit I am using and the finished marmalade I want to create. I like the whole fruit method for marmalades made with darker sugars, but also like to use it for my pink grapefruit marmalade, for optimum fruitiness and fleshy texture.

CITRUS FRUIT

All true marmalades contain citrus fruit and usually have the peel included. The bitter or Seville orange is the king of the citrus when it comes to marmalade-making. It has a thicker skin and more spongy pith than a regular orange; the pips are large and plentiful and the juice is quite sour, more like a lemon than an orange. It has a high pectin content, bringing a good set to marmalade. I use organic Seville oranges – I prefer to use fruit that I know hasn't been sprayed, as the peel is so integral to the recipe. Even so, I always give the fruit a light scrub under cold running water before I use it.

Frantically making a few batches of Seville orange marmalade when the oranges are in season is part of the appeal, but it seems a shame to restrict marmalade-making to only six weeks each year. There are lots of other citrus fruit to use during the other months. Whichever citrus you choose, use firm, fresh fruit. For best results it is preferable for the fruit to be slightly under-ripe or ripe, never over-ripe.

You can freeze Seville oranges; pectin is pretty resilient and most commercially made marmalade is made from pre-frozen orange flesh and/or peel. Long freezing can adversely affect the final set of the marmalade, though, so I try to use frozen Seville oranges within six months. I bag them up in 1kg quantities, which is the amount I need for a batch of classic Seville orange marmalade,

---

and freeze them. If, like me, you don't have a big freezer, cajole friends and family into storing them for you in return for a jar or two later in the year. I have bags of oranges squirrelled away in several borrowed freezers every year.

SUGARS

Sugar preserves marmalade. Granulated and demerara sugars are the most commonly used; caster sugar has a finer grain, which is ideal for baking but unnecessary for marmalade-making.

There are both preserving sugars and jam sugars on the market. Jam sugars have added pectin in them, and preserving sugar has larger crystals than granulated sugar – these dissolve more slowly so reduce stirring, and they froth less too. In general, I don't tend to use either of these but spend the extra pennies on unrefined cane sugars, which are cheaper anyway. I like the flavour they bring to my marmalade – if you taste a little white granulated sugar alongside a golden granulated sugar you will notice the difference: the golden sugar has caramel undertones and more depth of flavour. Using golden granulated sugar in a classic Seville orange marmalade will result in a slightly less bright jelly than if you use white granulated sugar, but it will be delicious and that, after all, is the most important thing. The exception is when I make marmalade from sweet oranges, when I use jam sugar to boost the pectin and setting qualities. I sometimes add soft dark brown

MARMALADE BASICS
Continued

---

sugars or treacle to add richness to marmalades – the varieties are endless.

Ideally, warm the sugar before you add it to the fruit and liquid. This prevents the temperature of the marmalade decreasing when the sugar is added, resulting in a shorter cooking time, which is preferable for flavour. However, on days when I'm using the oven for other things or I forget, I don't do this, and I have made lots and lots of delicious marmalade both ways. One thing not to forget, and absolutely crucial to success, is to ensure that all the sugar granules have dissolved before you turn up the heat and boil the marmalade to set it. Dissolving the sugar can take 15–20 minutes or longer in big batches, so be patient.

SHRED

The thickness of the shred I choose depends on the fruit I am using and the marmalade I am making. Shredding the peel before it is simmered means it cooks more quickly and evenly. For an elegant marmalade such as a classic Seville orange or a tangerine, lemon and lime, I prefer a fine to medium shred, but for a darker orange marmalade, a thicker, chunkier cut of peel seems right. I use these as general guidelines – a fine or thin cut shred is 1.5–3mm, a medium cut is 3–5mm, and a thick cut is more than 5mm and up to 8mm.

TO SOAK OR NOT TO SOAK?

For jelly marmalades, ideally soak Seville orange peel and other tough peels overnight before simmering them. It makes them quicker to cook. However, if you want to make Seville orange marmalade all in one day, it will still work perfectly well if you omit the soaking time.

STIRRING

Stir your marmalade now and then while the sugar is dissolving, to make sure it doesn't stick to the bottom of the pan or burn. Once the marmalade is at a rolling boil, there is no need to stir it. If you think it is catching, slowly drag a wooden spoon over the bottom of the pan rather than stirring enthusiastically.

A ROLLING BOIL

As soon as you have dissolved the sugar in the marmalade, you need to increase the heat and bring the mass to what is known as a rolling boil – there will be bubbles all over the surface of the marmalade, not just the edges, and it will bubble vigorously.

MARMALADE BASICS
Continued

SETTING POINT

Pectin is essential to make your marmalade set. Most of the pectin in citrus fruit is beneath the skin in the pith, but it is also in the pips and fruit membranes (think of it as the glue in your marmalade). Pectin works with the citrus fruit, sugar and acid in the marmalade to make it set. Sweet oranges have a lower pectin content than bitter oranges, so adding a pectin-rich fruit such as quince or Bramley cooking apple and/or lemon can help to achieve a good set. I sometimes use jam sugar with added pectin too.

The texture of marmalade varies, but none should be so stiff that they don't spread ('rock in a pot', as the experts call it!) A classic Seville orange should have a good jelly-like set; others such as lemon or blood orange will have a softer set unless you add extra pectin. I usually prefer not to, and to make marmalades with a range of textures. The amount of pectin in Seville oranges varies during their season, so it isn't unusual for setting times to vary slightly from batch to batch anyway. Don't expect the results to always be consistent – that is, after all, the difference between home cooking and manufacturing.

If the recipe involves a pouch with pith and pips in it that is suspended in the pan while the fruit and liquid simmer, press the pouch against the side of the pan with the back of a wooden spoon as you lift it out of the marmalade to ensure that any extra

---

pectin is extracted and goes back into your marmalade. It's a good idea to put the pouch into a bowl to cool slightly before giving it a final squeeze with your hands above the preserving pan before discarding it – wearing clean washing-up gloves makes this task less hazardous. It's the best way to make sure you have extracted every last bit of pectin.

Start testing for setting point after 15 minutes of boiling at a rolling boil. The setting point will vary depending on the batch size, the intensity of the rolling boil and the mixture of fruit.

You can test if your marmalade is set in several different ways. You can use a cook's sugar thermometer – the setting point of marmalade is 104.5°C and a thermometer can help to reassure the nervous first-time marmalade-maker. I do have one but don't always use it; it is useful but not essential.

Some marmalade-makers use the flake test. This involves dipping a wooden spoon into the marmalade, then holding it above the pan and turning it a few times. If the marmalade is set, it drops from the spoon as a flake or sheet of drips.

THE WRINKLE TEST

For me, by far the most reliable way to test for a set is to use the wrinkle test. I put a few saucers into the freezer before bringing the marmalade to a rolling boil, then, when I think my marmalade is at setting point, I turn the heat off under the pan (or reduce it to a very low setting), spoon a little hot marmalade on to one of the cold saucers from the freezer and leave it for a minute or so. If the marmalade is set, it will move slowly when you tilt the saucer and the surface will wrinkle when you push your finger into it. You will find that your finger will leave a little channel, which will then re-fill. If setting point hasn't been achieved, boil the marmalade for a further 5 minutes and repeat. As a rule, remember that it is preferable to have a softer-set marmalade than an overset one; you can always re-boil it to set it further.

SKIMMING

Traditionally, marmalade-makers add a small knob of butter to marmalade at the end of cooking to disperse the foamy scum (air bubbles) that is produced from boiling. I leave the marmalade to settle, off the heat, once it is at setting point, which helps the bubbles to subside, and a gentle stir – ideally in one direction – disperses any that are left. If there is excess, I skim it off with a spoon.

FILLING THE JARS AND STORING

Allowing the marmalade to settle for 15 minutes once it has reached setting point gives the shredded peel a chance to distribute evenly in the jelly before you fill the jars.

Make sure your jars are clean, dry and sterilised (see page 12) before filling. I line the jars up on a large baking tray so that any drips or splashes are contained – I find it impossible not to end up with some marmalade on the outside of the jars, no matter how carefully I fill them, and using a tray helps to avoid the stickiness being spread around the kitchen.

Fill the jars right to the top – you want to give as little opportunity as possible for air to get to your marmalade. The space between the marmalade and the lid is known as the headspace, and it shouldn't be more than a few millimetres. Cover the top of the marmalade with a waxed paper disc and a cellophane cover, or a tight-fitting lid.

I re-check the lids when the marmalade is cold and tighten them further. I find they usually also need a wipe with a hot, wet cloth at this stage. Store the jars in a cool dry place; marmalade keeps well for a couple of years.

MARMALADE BASICS
Continued

JARS AND LABELS –
A FEW RECOMMENDATIONS

JARS

Kilner jars – I like both the clip-on and the screw-top Kilner jars. See kilnerjar.co.uk for stockists.

Leifheit jars – a firm favourite, these come in 250ml to 1 litre sizes with screw-top lids. See leifheitus.com. They are often stocked in hardware stores and I have also bought them from philipmorrisdirect.co.uk.

Weck – these are simple and stylish, and I buy them whenever I spot them in a shop, as they aren't always the easiest to track down. See weckeurope.com.

jamjarshop.com – a good selection of jars of all shapes and sizes by mail order. Good value.

frenchflint.com – lots to choose from and lots of different styles of jar. Orders are collected or packed and posted to you.

etsy.com – a good source of vintage jars.

Also look in antique shops for vintage jars; I have a selection of French jars that I love. They don't have lids, so you have to use waxed discs and cellophane covers, but they are perfect for gifting.

Lakeland.co.uk – good for standard kit including preserving pans.

LABELS

Small brown luggage-style tags work well; I have bought them from stationers but coxandcox.com, Notonthehighstreet.com and etsy.com are also good sources.

Alternatively, cut out your own labels from different-coloured card. You can add reinforcement labels (the sticky self-adhesive circles that resemble a Polo mint) – they are available in most stationery shops and come in lots of different colours. Write the name of your marmalade or use a rubber stamp, then tie the tags around the top of your jars with string – plain or coloured.

You can print our set of marmalade labels from the following websites: saltyardbooks.co.uk or potofmarmalade.uk.

You can often find must-have labels at staples.co.uk – search for the Martha Stewart products. Marthastewart.com is great for creative ideas too. And, for adhesive labels – samanthabarnes.co.uk.

MARMALADE BASICS
Continued

What are you aiming for? Tender shreds of citrus peel evenly suspended in a jelly (clear or opaque) with a good balance of flavour and plenty of fruitiness.

The citrus peel must be soft before you add the sugar, otherwise you will end up with tough peel in your finished marmalade. It can take up to 1½–2 hours to soften; when it's ready you should be able to squeeze a piece of peel between two fingers, and it will break easily. In the finished marmalade, you are aiming for the peel to be soft enough that you can cut through it. It should be defined and hold texture but not be unpleasantly chewy.

The sugar must have completely dissolved before you increase the temperature under the pan to bring the marmalade to a rolling boil.

Don't leave the pan once you have brought the marmalade up to a rolling boil. Hot marmalade is sticky, and cleaning it off the hob isn't a fun pastime.

Once you have boiled the marmalade for 10–15 minutes, start to test for setting point: overcooking usually results in a sweet, overset, treacly marmalade that lacks fruitiness.

WHAT WENT WRONG?

The peel in my marmalade is hard and tough
It's likely that the peel wasn't soft enough before you added the sugar. Once the sugar is added it won't soften any further.

I used granulated sugar but the marmalade tastes very caramelly
The marmalade has probably been overcooked and some of the fresh fruit flavours have been lost; it should still be fine to eat. When using it in recipes, add a squeeze of lemon juice to compensate for the extra sweetness.

The texture of my marmalade is sugary
The sugar hadn't completely dissolved before you increased the heat for the marmalade to reach a rolling boil – it's really important that all the sugar has liquefied before you set the marmalade.

All the peel has sunk to the bottom of the jar
You may not have left your marmalade to settle once setting point was achieved, or the marmalade had not reached setting point before you potted it. If the latter is the case, the jelly won't be set sufficiently to suspend the shredded peel.

MARMALADE BASICS
Continued

My marmalade is too runny

You have probably under-boiled or really over-boiled it. If you have over-boiled the marmalade beyond its setting point, it is unlikely to ever set. If you have under-cooked it, you can re-boil it. A bit of an effort, I know, but worth a go. Tip the contents of your jars back into the preserving pan and bring the marmalade back to a rolling boil, testing it every 5 minutes to see when setting point has been reached. Adding a few spoonfuls of cooked Bramley apple or quince, a small raw Bramley apple, grated, or the juice of half a lemon before boiling will help the marmalade to set. Alternatively, you can use the un-set marmalade in recipes – ice creams, sauces and salad dressings are a good place to start.

My marmalade is solid

You have overcooked your marmalade. Taste it, and if it is good, don't waste it. Try adding a spoonful to stews, or add a little boiling water to thin the marmalade and mix with crème fraîche or cream and use as a sauce for hot puddings.

My marmalade has mould on the top

Micro-organisms are at work; make sure you sterilise your jars and lids properly next time before filling the warm jars with the hot marmalade, and make sure the headspace in the jar is minimal (see page 23). In my kitchen, as long as the mould is only on the top of the marmalade, I tend to scoop it off with a spoon, wipe around the inside of the rim of the jar with kitchen paper and eat the rest.

MARMALADE BASICS
Continued

GOOD THINGS TO KNOW

Keen to enter the marmalade awards? Go to dalemainmarmalade
awards.co.uk to find out more about the numerous categories
and how best to enter your jar. You will also find details of the
festival at Dalemain in Cumbria which kickstarts National
Marmalade Week each year.

Visit potofmarmalade.uk for more recipes and inspiration from my
kitchen and greedy travels.

COOKING WITH MARMALADE

Seville orange marmalade and its many variations work well in most recipes but, for quick reference, here are a few recipes that you might like to try using the more unusual varieties.

DARK AND MOODY MARMALADE

Marmalade harissa sausages
Toast and marmalade tart
Sticky ginger and marmalade parkin
Mini fat rascals
Figgy pudding Christmas cake
A mull for a cold winter's day
Whisky sour

FOUR FRUIT MARMALADE

Easy marmalade and sultana custard swirls
Toast and marmalade tart
A quick marmalade sauce
Sticky ginger and marmalade parkin
Mini fat rascals
Figgy pudding Christmas cake
A mull for a cold winter's day

QUINCE AND SWEET ORANGE MARMALADE

Overnight muesli with warm marmalade honey pears
Anna Del Conte's marmalade and apple crostata
Seville orange posset
Prune, orange and Armagnac bread and butter pudding
Quince Bakewell tarts
Marmalade fizz

SWEET ORANGE AND PASSION FRUIT MARMALADE

Tropical hotcakes
15-minute lemon passion fruit pots
Anna Del Conte's marmalade and apple crostata
Seville orange posset
Prune, orange and Armagnac bread and butter pudding

LEMON MARMALADES

Easy marmalade and sultana custard swirls
Gooey marmalade, pecan and cardamom buns
Persian spiced meatballs with dill yoghurt
Manchego fritters with chicory, orange and olives and a Seville
    orange dressing
Sticky barbecued teriyaki quail with chilled noodle salad

COOKING WITH MARMALADE
Continued

José Pizarro's griddled prawns with cauliflower purée and coriander

Vietnamese style caramel pork with a cucumber and peanut salad

Warm bulgar wheat and watercress salad with goat's curd and
    citrus dressing

Roast chicken with perry, apples and kumquats

Shoulder of lamb with quince, Iranian lime and a broad bean and
    pine nut pilaf

Sticky carrots with cider vinegar and bay

Christmas ham with cranberries and sloe gin

Sugar-cured duck with plums, orange and Marsala

Jerk-seasoned slow-roast shoulder of pork with pineapple

Toast and marmalade tart

15-minute lemon passion fruit pots

Queen of puddings with a twist

Cassata cheesecake

Mini lemon and blackcurrant puddings

Marmalade, ginger and Seville orange ice cream

Vin d'orange

Marmalade marguerite

A twist on a Cosmopolitan

Grapefruit, mint and lime punch

Whisky sour

LEMON AND LIMONCELLO MARMALADE

15-minute lemon passion fruit pots

LEMON AND BERGAMOT MARMALADE

Bergamot posset

LIME AND GRAPEFRUIT MARMALADE

Tropical hotcakes

Sticky barbecued teriyaki quail with chilled noodle salad

Vietnamese style caramel pork with a cucumber and peanut
    salad

Jerk-seasoned slow-roast shoulder of pork with pineapple

Queen of puddings with a twist

Coconut, papaya and grapefruit meringue roulade

Seville orange posset

A twist on a Cosmopolitan

Grapefruit, mint and lime punch

TANGERINE, LEMON AND LIME MARMALADE

Sticky barbecued teriyaki quail with chilled noodle salad
Aromatic slow-roast shoulder of pork with pineapple
Toast and marmalade tart
Seville orange posset
Marmalade fizz
Marmalade marguerite
A twist on a Cosmopolitan

PINK GRAPEFRUIT MARMALADE

Cassata cheesecake
A quick marmalade sauce
Coconut, papaya and grapefruit meringue roulade
Vin d'orange

THE
MARMALADE
COLLECTION

HOMEMADE
MARMALADE

CLASSIC SEVILLE ORANGE MARMALADE
Makes about 7 x 340ml jars

If you are short of time or have a sudden urge to make a batch of marmalade in one day, you can leave out the overnight soaking; it will just take longer to soften the peel before you add the sugar. As with all fruit, the weight of Seville oranges varies according to size, but, as a guide, 1kg is equal to 8–12 oranges. In addition to the three key ingredients – oranges, lemon and sugar – you will need some gauze or muslin.

1kg bitter Seville oranges
juice of 1 fat lemon
2kg granulated sugar

Put the radio on. Halve the oranges and, using the tip of a knife, flick out any obvious pips on to a double-layered square of gauze (or muslin), about 30 x 30cm. Squeeze the juice from the oranges into a very large bowl (or a large lidded plastic box), add any extra pips from the squeezer to the gauze and add any fleshy bits of orange to the bowl.

Now, cut each orange half into quarters and, using a knife, scrape out the membranes inside – put these and any more pips you find on to the gauze square. The next job is to shred the pithy peel as uniformly as possible into thin, medium or chunky shreds, as you wish; discard the buttons from the ends of the fruit as you go.

CLASSIC SEVILLE ORANGE MARMALADE
Continued

Transfer the shredded peel to the bowl too. Gather the gauze square together to form a money-bag shape, twist the top and tie it with string – an extra pair of hands comes in useful here. When you tie the string, leave one long end – you can use this to tie the gauze pouch on to the pan handle and immerse it in the liquid when you cook the peel. Put the pouch into the bowl to join the peel and juice. Add 2.25 litres of cold water, making sure everything is as immersed in the water as it can be, then cover with cling film (or a lid) and leave it overnight. I usually put the bowl in the cellar or garage.

The next day, tip everything from the bowl into a preserving pan and tie the gauze pouch to the pan handle so it sits on the base of the pan. Bring the whole lot to simmering point over a low–medium heat and simmer the peel until it is really soft – you should be able to squish it easily in your fingers; this will take about 1½ hours. The liquid will reduce as the peel simmers, and you will see a tidemark around the inside of the pan.

Once the peel is soft enough, remove the gauze pouch from the pan, pressing it against the side with the back of a wooden spoon as you do so to extract as much pectin as possible from the pith and pips – put the pouch into a bowl and leave it for 10 minutes to cool slightly.

Meanwhile, halve and squeeze the lemon and tip the lemon juice into the pan with the sugar; stir over a low heat. Give the gauze pouch a final squeeze to extract the last of the pectin into the marmalade; wearing clean washing-up gloves makes this easier. You can now discard the pouch, as its work is done.

Pre-heat the oven to 140°C/fan 120°C/gas1.

Keep stirring the marmalade from time to time to help dissolve the sugar. This is an important stage, so make sure all the sugar has dissolved before you move on to the next; it can take 15 minutes or so. I find that any pips I have missed usually pop to the surface at this point; scoop them out with a teaspoon. Put a few saucers in the freezer for the wrinkle test and put your jars and lids in the oven for 15–20 minutes to sterilise them.

Now, bring the marmalade up to a rolling boil and boil it for 20–25 minutes or until it has reached setting point – use the wrinkle test (see page 21). When the marmalade is ready, take the pan off the heat. Leave the marmalade to settle for 15 minutes; this will help to distribute the peel evenly and make it less hazardous to pot. Give it a gentle stir in one direction to disperse any air bubbles.

Using a measuring jug and a funnel, transfer your marmalade into hot sterilised jars. Seal and leave the marmalade to cool completely.

CLASSIC SEVILLE ORANGE MARMALADE
Continued

Give the jars a second wipe over with a hot cloth and dry them before labelling. Store the jars of golden marmalade in a dry, cool place, where it will keep for at least a year.

ALSO TRY ...

Ginger and rum marmalade – add 75–100g of finely chopped root ginger when you add the sugar. Add 50ml of dark rum once the sugar has dissolved, boil to set, then add another 2 tablespoons of dark rum once the marmalade has reached setting point.

Black treacle marmalade – add 2 tablespoons of black treacle with the sugar; the treacle adds a gorgeous richness.

Spiced marmalade – add 6 star anise and 10 bruised cardamom pods to the gauze pouch with the pith and pips. Add a fresh star anise and a couple of cardamom pods (lightly squash them first) to each jar when potting the marmalade.

Tonka bean marmalade – this South American bean is small, flat, black and wrinkled, but don't let its looks deceive you; it has a wonderful vanilla flavour. Add 3 tonka beans to the gauze pouch with the pith and pips.

Double orange marmalade – add 50ml of Cointreau once the sugar has dissolved, boil to set, then add another 2 tablespoons of Cointreau once the marmalade has reached setting point.

DARK AND MOODY MARMALADE
Makes 8 x 340g jars

A dark chunky marmalade made by the whole fruit method. This
has a treacly flavour and all the rich characteristics of an Oxford-
style marmalade – first created at Frank Cooper's Oxford shop in
the nineteenth century. The recipe also works well with 2kg of
granulated sugar instead of the demerara and muscovado mix,
and the whisky is, of course, optional.

1kg bitter Seville oranges
4 lemons
1.75kg demerara sugar
250g dark muscovado sugar
50ml whisky

Put the whole oranges into a saucepan and cover them with
water. Bring to simmering point, then simmer them, covered, for
1½–2 hours, or until the oranges are really soft; they should give
no resistance when pierced with the tip of a small sharp knife.
Halve the lemons and squeeze the juice.

Remove the hot oranges from the pan to a bowl (I use tongs to do
this), and tip the cooking liquid into a measuring jug.

DARK AND MOODY MARMALADE
Continued

When the oranges are cool enough to handle, pierce them at one end and squeeze the excess juice into the measuring jug – there won't be a lot but it saves the precious liquid from running all over your chopping board.

Now quarter the oranges and slice them, removing the buttons from the ends of the fruit; I like 3–6mm slices for this marmalade. Put the fleshy orange slices into a preserving pan as they are ready and add any escaped juice to the liquid in the jug. Discard the pips.

You want the liquid in the jug to be 1.5 litres, so adjust accordingly, topping it up with extra water if need be, then add that to the pan with the lemon juice and sugars.

Heat the marmalade over a low heat, stirring to dissolve the sugar. When all the sugar has dissolved, bring everything up to a rolling boil. Boil the marmalade for 30–35 minutes or until setting point is reached (see page 20).

Take the pan off the heat and gently stir in the whisky, then leave the marmalade to settle for 15 minutes before transferring to hot sterilised jars (see page 12). Seal and leave to cool.

A Pot of Marmalade

MARMALADE MADE IN THE PRESSURE COOKER

Makes 6 x 340g jars

I knew Seville oranges could be cooked in a pressure cooker, but hadn't tried it until a recipe came my way from Frances Howe, aged 102, who makes marmalade every year; it's a family ritual. The pressure cooker method is good for speed and ease and makes a bright, fresh-tasting marmalade. The recipe also works well as a half batch if you want to make a few jars; just remember to halve the two lots of water too; the cooking times remain the same.

900g bitter Seville oranges
4 lemons
1.75kg golden granulated sugar
a small knob of butter

Remove and discard the buttons from the oranges, then halve the fruit. Flick out as many of the pips as possible into a pressure cooker, then squeeze the oranges and tip the juice into a large measuring jug, along with any pulp on the juicer. Cut the orange shells into quarters, scrape out the pith and add this along with any remaining pips to the pressure cooker.

MARMALADE MADE IN THE PRESSURE COOKER
Continued

Squeeze the lemons and add the lemon juice to the measuring jug. Put any pips and the chopped shells of two of the lemons into the pressure cooker with 300ml of water (you can discard the other lemon shells). Put the lid on, bring to pressure and cook for 6 minutes. Meanwhile, start to shred the orange peel.

Release the pressure from the cooker and empty half the contents into a sieve set over the jug of juice. Leave it to drain, then press with the back of a spoon to extract as much of the pectin as possible, remembering to scrape any goodness from under the sieve, then discard the contents of the sieve and repeat with the other half.

Put the shredded peel into the pressure cooker with 900ml of water. Lock the lid, bring to pressure and cook for 17 minutes.

Tip the sugar and all the juice from the measuring jug into a preserving pan and add the small knob of butter and the peel, as soon as it is ready. Slowly bring the contents of the preserving pan to a rolling boil, then boil the marmalade for 15 minutes, or until setting point has been reached (see page 20).

Take the pan off the heat and leave the marmalade to settle for 15 minutes before transferring to hot sterilised jars (see page 12). Seal and leave to cool.

SWEET ORANGE AND PASSION FRUIT MARMALADE

Makes 5 x 340g jars

The passion fruit adds an irresistible fragrance to this marmalade and a little acidity to balance the sweet oranges.

---

3 lemons
750–850g (3–4) sweet oranges
500g (2–3) Bramley cooking apples
650g (8 large) passion fruit
1kg jam sugar

Halve and squeeze the lemons, then tip the juice into a small bowl, adding the pips and any flesh from the squeezer. Chop the lemon shells and add these to the bowl too. Add enough water to cover, about 100ml, and set aside.

Discard the buttons from the oranges, then put the oranges into a medium pan, cover with water and bring to the boil. Cover and simmer for 1½ hours, or until soft when pierced with a small sharp knife.

Meanwhile, peel and core the apples, chop them into medium pieces and put them into a small saucepan with 5 tablespoons of water. Simmer the apple, partially covered, for 10–15 minutes, or until fluffy – give it a stir from time to time and add a splash more water if needed. Halve the passion fruit and sieve the pulp into a bowl, massaging the seeds with the back of the spoon in the sieve to get as much juice as possible. Remember to scrape any juice from the bottom of the sieve, then discard the seeds – you should have about 125ml of passion fruit juice.

Lift the oranges out of the pan, reserving the cooking liquid. When the oranges are cool enough to handle, quarter them and slice each quarter into 3–5mm slices, discarding any pips. Transfer the slices and any orange juice to a preserving pan.

Drain the bowl with the lemon pieces into a measuring jug and discard the lemon debris. Add enough of the orange cooking liquid to the measuring jug to make the total up to 750ml; you can discard the rest. Add the liquid to the pan along with the sugar and cooked apple, and stir together.

Heat the marmalade over a low heat, stirring, to dissolve the sugar. Add the passion fruit juice and bring the marmalade to a rolling boil, then boil the marmalade for 20 minutes, or until it has reached setting point (see page 20) – remember that this marmalade is made with jam sugar, so don't overcook it or it will be too solid.

Leave the marmalade to settle for 15 minutes before transferring to hot sterilised jars (see page 12). Seal, then leave to cool.

ALSO TRY …

Sweet orange and lavender marmalade – replace the passion fruit pulp with 1 tablespoon of dried lavender buds; you can usually find these alongside other jars of dried herbs and spices in stores.

QUINCE AND SWEET ORANGE MARMALADE
Makes 4 x 340g jars

Quince and marmalade have been linked since ancient times, and the high pectin content of tart-flavoured apples has been used to help set marmalades as far back as the seventeenth century, when Pippin apples were favoured. Sweet oranges contain less pectin than bitter Seville oranges, so they need a little extra help to set; I use quince and cooking apples to do the job and there is no greater cooking apple than the Bramley.

500g (2–3) sweet oranges
350g (1–2) quince
200g (1 small) Bramley cooking apple
3 lemons
1kg golden granulated sugar

Preheat the oven to 170°C/fan 150°C/gas 3. Remove and discard the buttons from the oranges, then put the fruit into a smallish pan, cover with water and bring to the boil. Cover the pan and simmer the oranges for 1½ hours, or until soft when pierced with a small sharp knife.

Quarter and core the quince (don't peel), then slice into chunky wedges and put into a small baking dish. Peel and core the apple, cut that into chunks too, and add to the dish – the fruit should fit quite snugly. Add 300ml of water, then bake the fruit, uncovered, for about 2 hours or until the quince is tender.

Purée the quince and the fluffy apple in a food processor – if there is a little liquid left in the baking dish, add that too. If not, add a tablespoon of water.

Lift the oranges out of the pan, reserving the cooking liquid. When they are cool enough to handle, quarter them. Then slice each quarter – I aim for 3–5mm shreds. Transfer the fleshy sliced oranges and the quince purée to a preserving pan.

Squeeze the lemons (keep the shells) and pour the juice into a measuring jug. Add enough of the reserved orange cooking liquid to make the total amount up to 750ml, topping it up with water if necessary. Add the liquid to the pan with the sugar.

Roughly chop the lemon shells in the food processor, then tip them on to a double-layered square of gauze (or muslin). Gather the square together to form a money-bag shape, twist the top and tie it with string. Leave one end long enough to be able to tie the pouch to the pan handle so it is submerged in the liquid.

Heat the marmalade over a low heat, stirring to dissolve the sugar. As soon as all the sugar has dissolved, increase the heat and bring the marmalade to a rolling boil. Boil the marmalade for 15 minutes, or until it has reached setting point (see page 20). Transfer to hot sterilised jars (see page 12), seal and allow to cool.

LEMON SUNSHINE MARMALADE
Makes 8 x 340g jars

Fresh, zesty and full of kitchen sunshine, this marmalade will perk
up the gloomiest of winter days. The bicarbonate of soda helps
the acidic mix to set, a tip given to me by expert Robert Parker
of Wilkin & Sons, makers of Tiptree marmalade.

200g (1 small) Bramley cooking apple
1.4kg (11–12) lemons
2kg golden granulated sugar
1 teaspoon bicarbonate of soda

Peel and core the apple, putting the peelings and core on
to a double-layered square of gauze (or muslin). Chop the
apple into small pieces and put them into a small saucepan with
4 tablespoons of water. Simmer, partially covered, for 10–15
minutes, or until fluffy and smooth – give the apple a stir from
time to time and add a splash more water if needed.

Meanwhile, halve the lemons, then squeeze them and tip the
lemon juice into a measuring jug; flick the pips on to the gauze
square and add any pulp from the squeezer to the juice.

Cut the lemon halves into quarters and shred the peel with the
inner membranes intact – I tend to remove the buttons and the
knobbly ends from the lemons before I start shredding and add

---

these to the gauze square along with any rogue pips. As the peel is ready, scoop it up into a large bowl.

Add enough water to the juice to make it up to a total of 1.5 litres. Add the liquid to the bowl with the shredded peel.

Gather the gauze square together to form a money-bag shape, twist the top and tie it with string. Leave one end of the string long enough to be able to tie it on to the side of the preserving pan later. Put this pouch into the bowl too, submerging it in the liquid. Cover the bowl and leave everything to soak overnight. Cool the cooked apple, then put it into a separate bowl, cover and chill.

The next day, tip the whole lot into a preserving pan, including the cooked apple. Tie the gauze pouch to the side of the pan. Bring everything to the boil, then reduce the heat and simmer the peel gently for 30–45 minutes, or until it is really tender, giving it a stir from time to time. Remove the pouch, squeezing it well against the side of the pan to extract as much pectin as possible.

Tip the sugar into the pan – the marmalade will feel very thick, but keep it over a very low heat, stirring until all the sugar has dissolved. Now take the pan off the heat, stir in the bicarbonate of soda, then return the pan to the heat. Keep an eye on the marmalade when you add the soda and heat it, as it bubbles vigorously initially.

LEMON SUNSHINE MARMALADE
Continued

Increase the heat and bring the marmalade to a rolling boil, then boil the marmalade for 20–25 minutes, or until it has reached setting point (see page 20). Leave the marmalade to settle for 15 minutes, then transfer it to hot sterilised jars (see page 12), seal and leave to cool.

ALSO TRY ...

Lemon and gin marmalade – add 50ml of gin with the bicarbonate of soda, boil to set, then add another 2 tablespoons of gin once the marmalade has reached setting point.

Lemon and limoncello marmalade – add 50ml of limoncello with the bicarbonate of soda, boil to set, then add another 2 tablespoons of limoncello once the marmalade has reached setting point.

Lemon and bergamot marmalade – the bergamot is a natural cross between an orange and a lemon. It is grown in Calabria in Italy and the peel is used to flavour Earl Grey tea. I was warned by Calabrian chef Francesco Mazzei how bitter the peel is, and after two attempts of making a marmalade using it, I realised I should have taken more notice. However, the juice is delicious – similar to lemon juice but with a fragrant, floral note.

Make as the master recipe but use only 800g (8 or 9 lemons) and add 300ml of bergamot juice to the lemon juice; depending on which of three varieties you find and the size of the fruit, this will probably mean you need 4 or 5 bergamot fruit. Discard the bergamot pips and shells and continue the recipe as above, making the total liquid up to 1.5 litres. When you have simmered the peel until tender, turn off the heat and gently stir in 2 Earl Grey tea bags. Leave to infuse for 30 minutes, stirring now and then. Remove the tea bags and the gauze pouch and reheat the marmalade before tipping in the sugar and, once that has dissolved, the bicarbonate of soda; then finish the recipe as above.

SICILIAN LEMON MARMALADE
Makes 4 x 340g jars

I was lucky enough to spend a beautiful sunny day at one of the
most stunning villas in Sicily, Don Arcangelo all'Olmo, near Mount
Etna, one summer. The owner, Marina di San Giuliano, is a
wonderful cook and this is my adaptation of a recipe from her
family cookbook. The villa is surrounded by lemon groves and
Marina uses the fragrant Sicilian lemons to make this delightful
marmalade. It has a more pulpy texture than traditional
marmalade and has become a firm favourite.

1kg (9–10) lemons, regular or, ideally, Sicilian or Amalfi lemons
850g golden granulated sugar
1 teaspoon vanilla extract
50ml Cognac (or Armagnac)

Prick the skin of the lemons – I use the tip of a small sharp knife;
then put them into a large bowl. Cover them with cold water, then
put a plate on top to keep them weighted down. Leave the
lemons for 3 days, changing the water each day. This will help get
rid of any excess bitterness.

Take the lemons out of the water, quarter them, and cut them
into thin slices; discard the pips. Put the lemon slices into a large
non-stick pan or flameproof casserole – I use one that has a
24–25cm base diameter. Bring to simmering point, then leave the
lemon slices to simmer gently in their own juice, covered with a

---

A Pot of Marmalade

lid, for 1½ hours. Keep an eye on them as they cook and stir them frequently – I find after 30–45 minutes I need to add a cup of water from time to time to prevent them sticking. It will all depend on how juicy your lemons are to start with. When the lemon slices have reduced to a pulp, the consistency is similar to thick custard and the peel is soft, it's time to add the sugar.

Stir in the sugar and continue to cook the marmalade over a low heat for a further 45 minutes to an hour. The final consistency should be similar to stewed apple. Keep stirring it to prevent it sticking – if it does, add a touch more water.

When you have obtained the right density, remove the pan from the heat and stir in the vanilla extract and the Cognac. Transfer the marmalade to hot sterilised jars (see page 12), seal and leave to cool.

LIME AND GRAPEFRUIT MARMALADE
Makes 5 x 340g jars

This has a lovely fresh, fruity flavour and can be made at any time of year.

1kg (14) limes
2 white grapefruit
1 lemon
1.5kg golden granulated sugar

First, halve and squeeze the juice from 8 of the limes, both grapefruit and the lemon. Keep the fruit shells and flick any pips on to a large double-layered square of gauze (or muslin) as you go. Pour the juice into a measuring jug, adding any flesh from the juicer.

Now cut each grapefruit half into four and, using the flat side of a sharp knife or a spoon, remove the membrane from each piece and put this on the gauze square too. You will be left with the grapefruit peel with its layer of spongy white pith attached; shred the peel with this intact, as finely as you can.

Top up the juice in the jug with water to make 1.5 litres. Cut up the shells of the limes and the lemon into smallish pieces – either by hand or in a food processor – then tip these on to the gauze square. Gather the gauze square together to make a money-bag shape, twist the top and tie it with string. Leave one end long enough to be able to attach the pouch to the side of the pan. Put the shredded peel and the liquid into the pan, pushing the pouch into the liquid as much as possible.

Simmer the peel until tender, about 20–25 minutes. Meanwhile, halve and squeeze the remaining 6 limes – you can discard the shells. When the peel is tender, lift the gauze pouch out of the pan, squeezing it against the side of the pan with the back of a wooden spoon as you do so to ensure any goodness goes back into the marmalade, then discard it.

Tip the sugar into the pan, add the freshly squeezed lime juice, and stir over a low heat until the sugar has dissolved. Now increase the heat, bring the marmalade to a rolling boil and boil it for 15 minutes, or until it has reached setting point (see page 20). Leave the marmalade to settle for 15 minutes before transferring it to hot sterilised jars (see page 12); seal, then cool.

ALSO TRY ...

Lime, grapefruit and elderflower marmalade – use 800g (11) limes in the recipe and instead of adding the juice of 6 limes with the sugar, add the juice of 3 limes with 75ml of elderflower cordial, homemade for the best flavour.

TANGERINE, LEMON AND LIME MARMALADE
Makes 6 x 340g jars

This is so pretty with its three-way mix of coloured peel. A bit time-consuming to prepare, but well worth it.

---

6 lemons
1kg (9–10) tangerines (or same weight of mandarins or
    clementines)
4 limes
1.35kg golden granulated sugar

Using a vegetable peeler, pare the peel off the lemons in strips, leaving the white pith behind; keep the strips to one side. Next, cut all the lemons, tangerines and limes in half and squeeze the juice into a large bowl, adding the fleshy bits of fruit from the squeezer. Keep any pips you find and put them into a medium-sized bowl.

Now, quarter the tangerine and lime halves and use a sharp knife to scrape out the inner membranes from the peel; use the flat blade of the knife to do this rather than the pointed end. Remove and discard the buttons from the ends of the fruit as you go.

Add the fruit membranes to the bowl of pips. Chop the shells of the lemons and put them into this bowl too, along with 500ml of cold water – the water should cover as much of the fruit bits and bobs as possible. I put a small plate inside the top of the bowl on top of the fruit to help weight them down.

Thinly shred the reserved strips of lemon peel, followed by the tangerine and lime peel, then put all the shredded citrus peel into the large bowl with the juice and add 1 litre of water. Cover both bowls and leave them overnight. I usually put them in the cellar or garage.

The following day, tip the contents of the large bowl into a preserving pan. Drain the liquid from the smaller bowl and add that too. Put the membrane, pith and pips on to a double-layered square of gauze (or muslin), then gather the gauze together to form a money-bag shape, twist the top and tie it with string. Leave one end of the string long enough to be able to tie the pouch to the pan handle and immerse it in the liquid.

Bring the liquid to the boil and simmer the peel, uncovered, for 45 minutes to 1 hour – you want the peel to be soft enough to squash between two fingers.

Take the pan off the heat. Remove the gauze pouch, pressing it against the side of the pan with the back of a wooden spoon to extract any pectin – put it into a bowl to cool for 10 minutes or so, then give it a final squeeze with your hands and discard it.

TANGERINE, LEMON AND LIME MARMALADE
Continued

Tip the sugar into the pan and put it back over a low heat, stirring until it has all dissolved. Then increase the heat and bring the marmalade to a rolling boil. Boil the marmalade for 15 minutes, or until setting point is reached (see page 20) – this marmalade, made with tangerines, reaches setting point quickly. Leave it to settle for 15 minutes before transferring to hot sterilised jars (see page 12). Seal and cool.

FOUR FRUIT MARMALADE
Makes 9 x 340g jars

A chunky marmalade with bags of fruity flavour which often
proves to be a very popular choice with men.

500g bitter Seville oranges
2 pink or ruby red grapefruit
3 lemons
1 sweet orange
2.25kg golden granulated sugar

Put all the whole fruit except the sweet orange into a preserving
pan and add water to cover. If you have one, place a large
saucepan lid on top of the fruit to keep it submerged. Either way,
bring to the boil, then reduce the heat and simmer the fruit for
1½–2 hours, or until tender – you should be able to pierce the
skins easily with the point of a small sharp knife.

Lift the fruit out of the pan (tip the cooking water into a bowl)
and when it is cool enough to handle, pierce the ends of all
the fruit and gently squeeze out the excess juice into a large
measuring jug – this avoids the juice running all over the board.

Now, slice all the peel with the flesh intact, adding any excess juice
to the measuring jug and discarding the buttons from the fruit. I
cut the oranges and lemons into quarters first and the grapefruit
into eighths before slicing them. I aim for a 3–5mm shred. Flick out

FOUR FRUIT MARMALADE
Continued

(and discard) the pips into a small bowl as you go and return all the sliced fleshy fruit to the preserving pan. Fish out any pips from the juice in the measuring jug too.

Squeeze the sweet orange and add the juice and any fleshy bits from the squeezer to the measuring jug. Next, add enough of the fruit cooking water to the jug to make a total of 1.5 litres – make up the difference with water if necessary.

Tip this liquid and the sugar into the preserving pan along with any juice that has formed around the pips in the bowl – you can discard the pips now.

Heat the marmalade over a low heat, stirring to dissolve all the sugar. Bring the marmalade to a rolling boil and boil it for 35–45 minutes, or until the marmalade has reached setting point (see page 20).

Take the pan off the heat and leave the marmalade to settle for 15 minutes before transferring to hot sterilised jars (see page 12). Seal and leave to cool.

PINK GRAPEFRUIT MARMALADE
Makes 6 x 340g jars

I have experimented and made this marmalade by both the jelly
and the whole fruit methods, and I prefer the whole fruit, which
makes a marmalade with the fullest, fleshiest grapefruit flavour. It
is also a gorgeous pinky red colour.

---

3 pink or ruby red grapefruit
4 lemons
1.75kg golden granulated sugar

Put the whole grapefruit into a medium saucepan, cover with
water and bring to the boil. Then reduce the heat, put a lid on the
pan and simmer the fruit for 1½ hours, or until tender when
pierced with the end of a small sharp knife.

Lift the grapefruit out of the hot liquid, reserving the cooking
liquid, and leave them to cool until you can handle them
comfortably. Halve the grapefruit, then cut the halves into
sections and slice these. Put the fleshy slices and any juice into
a preserving pan, discarding any pips you find.

Halve and squeeze the lemons, discarding the shells, then pour
the juice into a measuring jug and add enough of the reserved
grapefruit cooking water to make the total up to 1.25 litres. Add
this liquid and the sugar to the preserving pan.

PINK GRAPEFRUIT MARMALADE
Continued

Gently heat and stir over a low flame to dissolve all the sugar. Then bring the marmalade to a rolling boil and boil it for 20–25 minutes, or until it reaches setting point (see page 20). Leave the marmalade to settle for 15 minutes before transferring to hot sterilised jars (see page 12). Seal, then leave to cool.

BLOOD ORANGE AND VANILLA MARMALADE
Makes 6 x 340g jars

Blood oranges are such a wonderfully sweet and fragrant citrus fruit, particularly Sicilian blood oranges, which are in season in January and February.

800g (6–7) blood oranges
400g (1–2) Bramley cooking apples
4 lemons
2 limes
2kg golden granulated sugar
2 vanilla pods

Remove and discard the buttons from the oranges, then put the oranges into a medium pan, cover with water and bring to the boil. Reduce the heat, put a lid on the pan and simmer for 1 hour, or until tender when pierced with a small sharp knife.

Meanwhile, peel and core the apples, and put the peelings and cores on to a large double-layered square of gauze (or muslin). Chop the apples into small pieces and put these into a pan with 5 tablespoons of water. Simmer, partially covered, for 10minutes, or until fluffy, stir the apples from time to time and add a splash more water if needed.

BLOOD ORANGE AND VANILLA MARMALADE
Continued

Lift the oranges out of the pan, reserving the cooking liquid. When they are cool enough to handle, halve and slice them – I aim for 3–5mm slices and usually quarter the halves first. Transfer the sliced fleshy oranges, and any blood orange juice that accumulates, into a preserving pan, flicking any pips on to the gauze square.

Zest the lemons into the pan and halve, then squeeze them, and squeeze the limes too. Pour the lemon and lime juice into a measuring jug, adding any pulp from the squeezer. Chop the shells of the lemons and limes. Put any pips and the chopped shells of the lemons and limes on to the gauze – you can whiz the shells in a food processor if you don't want to have to chop them by hand. Add enough of the orange cooking liquid to the measuring jug to make the total up to 1 litre; you can discard the rest.

Add the liquid, sugar and the cooked apple to the preserving pan. Slit the vanilla pods in half lengthways and widthways and scrape out the seeds, then put the seeds and the pods into the pan. Gather the gauze square together to form a money-bag shape, twist the top and tie with string. Leave one long end and tie this to the side of the pan so it touches the bottom.

Heat the marmalade over a low heat, stirring, to dissolve the sugar. Remove the gauze pouch, squeezing it against the side of the pan as you do so. Now, bring the marmalade to a rolling boil and boil it for 20–25 minutes, or until setting point is reached (see page 20).

Leave the marmalade to settle for 10–15 minutes before transferring to hot sterilised jars (see page 12). You can remove the pieces of vanilla pod if you prefer, but I tend to leave them in. Seal and leave to cool.

KUMQUAT AND CRANBERRY MARMALADE
Makes 5 x 340g jars

You can usually buy the very first of the bitter Seville oranges
from specialist grocers just before Christmas, when the first
exports arrive from Spain. If you find them, this marmalade makes
ideal Christmas presents.

375g bitter Seville oranges
2 lemons
2 cinnamon sticks
450g kumquats
1kg demerara sugar
100g dried cranberries

Remove the buttons from the oranges, then halve and squeeze
them; flick out the pips on to a small double-layered square of
gauze (or muslin) and pour the juice into a preserving pan. Now
quarter the halves and shred them, including the pith. Put the
pithy peel into the pan.

Halve and squeeze the lemons, adding the pips to the gauze
square and the juice to the pan. Chop the lemon shells and add
those to the gauze too.

Add 1.75 litres of water to the pan. Gather the gauze square
together to make a money-bag shape, twist the top and tie it with
string. Leave one end of the string long enough to be able to

attach the pouch to the side of the preserving pan and immerse it in the liquid. Now tie up the cinnamon sticks in another small double-layered square of gauze and immerse this in the liquid too; no need to tie this one to the pan, just stir the mix from time to time to make sure the cinnamon sticks are flavouring the whole batch. Bring everything to simmering point and simmer for 45 minutes.

Meanwhile, slice the kumquats into rounds, discarding any pips and little buttons as you go. After the 45 minutes, add the kumquats to the pan, pushing them down into the liquid, and simmer for a further 45 minutes or until all the peel is tender.

Remove the gauze bags, pressing the one with the pips and the chopped lemon shells against the side of the pan with the back of a wooden spoon as you lift it out before discarding it. Add the sugar to the pan and stir the marmalade over a low heat until all the sugar has dissolved. Then bring everything to a rolling boil and boil the marmalade for 10–15 minutes, or until setting point is reached (see page 20).

Stir in the cranberries, leave the marmalade to settle for 15 minutes, then transfer to hot sterilised jars (see page 12). Seal and cool.

APPLE HARVEST MARMALADE

Makes 12 x 340g jars

This recipe was given to me by Jane Hasell-McCosh, originator of
the World's Original Marmalade Awards. It was developed when
there was a bumper harvest of apples in Jane's Cumbrian garden. I
grew up with a garden with several apple trees and in the autumn
Dad frequently stood at the back door, smiling, arms laden with
yet more apples, while my mother pondered new creative recipes.
This recipe will be a godsend to anyone with the same dilemma.
Jane's favourite apple to use is Scotch Bridget, which is a Scottish
cooking apple. Bramley apples make a very good substitute. This
recipe makes a generous quantity – you can of course halve it, but
remember to halve the water quantity too.

---

2 white grapefruit
4 lemons
900g (4–5) Bramley cooking apples
2.25kg golden granulated sugar

Cut the grapefruit and lemons in half, discarding the buttons from
the ends. Put the fruit into a preserving pan.

Peel, quarter and core the apples, and put the cores and peel on
to a double-layered square of gauze (or muslin). Put the apple
quarters into the pan. Gather the gauze square together to form
a money-bag shape and tie it at the top with string, leaving one
end long enough to tie the pouch to the side of the pan and

---

immerse it in the liquid. Add 3 litres of water and bring the whole lot to simmering point, then simmer the fruit gently for 1½ hours, or until the citrus are tender – you should be able to pierce the skin with the tip of a small sharp knife without resistance. I sometimes put a plate on top of the fruit at the beginning to keep the fruit immersed.

Lift the fruit out of the pan with a slotted spoon and into a bowl, allowing any juice to run back into the pan. Leave the fruit until it is cool enough to handle.

Lift the gauze pouch out of the pan, squeezing it against the side as you do so to get all the goodness out, and put it into a bowl. Cut the fruit into quarters or smaller pieces, then slice it, discarding any pips you come across. Drain the liquid that is left in the pan through a coarse sieve and into a bowl; again, discard any pips. Return the liquid to the preserving pan along with any fleshy fruit that is in the sieve; add the sliced fruit and the sugar too. Give the gauze pouch a final squeeze over the pan, then discard it.

Heat the marmalade over a low flame, stirring, until the sugar has dissolved. Then bring it to a rolling boil and boil for 20–30 minutes, or until setting point is reached (see page 20).

Leave the marmalade to settle for 15 minutes, then transfer to hot sterilised jars (see page 12), seal and leave to cool.

BREAKFAST
&
BRUNCH

A SIMPLE SEEDED LOAF FOR MARMALADE ON TOAST
Makes I Loaf

Even if you have never made bread before, this is really easy to make and is delicious toasted, spread with butter and marmalade. If you like lots of seeds, add 3 tablespoons to the dough mix too; just mix them into the flour with the sugar, yeast and salt.

25g butter
175g strong white flour
300g strong wholemeal flour
I tablespoon caster sugar
I teaspoon fast-action dried yeast
a little oil
I small egg
mixed seeds such as sunflower, pumpkin and linseed, for
     sprinkling on top

Put the butter into a measuring jug and add 275ml of boiling water from the kettle. Stir, then leave the butter to melt and the liquid to cool until it is just lukewarm.

Tip both types of flour into a large bowl with the sugar, yeast and a teaspoon of salt. Stir together.

A SIMPLE SEEDED LOAF FOR MARMALADE ON TOAST
Continued

Make a well in the centre of the flour. Give the buttery water a stir (you should be able to hold your little finger in it without any discomfort), then pour it into the well. Mix with a large spoon, then bring the dough together with your hands, incorporating any drier bits into it. Now knead the dough by hand for 10 minutes, or in a free-standing mixer with a dough attachment for 5 minutes. When the dough is ready, it will spring back when you gently press your finger into it.

Put the dough into a clean, lightly oiled bowl, cover with oiled cling film, and leave it to rise in a warm place away from draughts. You are aiming for it to double in size – this will take about 1½ hours.

When the dough has risen, punch it a couple of times with your fist to expel the air and knead it again for a couple of minutes, then put into a lightly oiled 19 x 9 x 7cm loaf tin. Leave the dough, uncovered, to rise, this time for 45 minutes or until well risen in the tin. Meanwhile, preheat the oven to 240°C/fan 220°C/gas 9.

Lightly beat the egg in a cup with a pinch of salt and use it to brush the top of the loaf, then sprinkle the top with seeds. Put the tin into the oven and immediately reduce the temperature to 220°C/fan 200°C/gas 7. Bake the loaf for 30 minutes. Cool in the tin for 15 minutes, then tip it out on to a wire rack to continue cooling.

PADDINGTON'S MARMALADE SANDWICHES
Serves 1

Everyone knows that Paddington Bear is extremely fond of a marmalade sandwich, and I think that they are very good for a breakfast-on-the-run. One of my favourite childhood books was *A Bear Called Paddington,* which includes the memorable moment when Paddington accidentally knocks a marmalade sandwich from the ledge of a theatre box on to the head of an unsuspecting patron below.

Michael Bond, author of *Paddington*, has generously agreed to share Paddington's very special tips for the best marmalade sandwiches. Here they are...

---

1. First choose your marmalade – not too solid, but not so runny that it comes through the holes in the bread (Mrs Bird's is the very best).

2. The secret of success is in the chunks – not too thin, and not too thick.

3. Most important of all – I keep my sandwiches under my hat for several days.

4. Moderation in all things, though, so I never keep more than four sandwiches there at once.

SEVILLE ORANGE BRIOCHE
Makes 1 Loaf

I leave my butter out of the fridge overnight, as it really does need to be soft when it is added to this dough. Spread thick slices of brioche with soft butter and a thin layer of marmalade. It is also good lightly toasted and served with meaty pâtés or terrines.

---

2 tablespoons (30ml) milk

225g strong plain flour, plus extra for dusting

1 x 7g sachet of fast-action dried yeast

1 teaspoon ground cinnamon

1 teaspoon ground ginger

2 tablespoons caster sugar

4 tablespoons Seville orange marmalade

2 large eggs

150g very soft unsalted butter, plus a little extra for greasing

TO FINISH

1 small egg

1–2 tablespoons crystallised ginger pieces

1 teaspoon cinnamon sugar (or granulated sugar)

Heat the milk until just warm (you should be able to hold your little finger in it without any discomfort). Tip the flour into the bowl of a free-standing food mixer with a dough attachment and stir in the yeast, spices, sugar and a teaspoon of salt.

Put the marmalade into a jug. If it contains large pieces of peel, chop them – I use scissors to do this. Add the eggs and warm milk and whisk with a fork to combine. Pour the liquid into the flour and mix with a spoon initially, then knead with the mixer dough hook on a low speed for 10 minutes.

Now add the butter, a small piece at a time, still mixing. Once combined, scrape the soft dough into a lightly buttered bowl, cover with a damp tea towel and refrigerate overnight.

The next day, take the dough out of the fridge and set it aside for an hour. Lightly butter a 19 x 9 x 7cm loaf tin.

Tip the dough on to a floured work surface and dust the dough lightly with flour too – it will still be really soft but that is how it should be. Carefully form it into an oval shape and transfer it to the buttered tin. Cover loosely with oiled cling film and leave it for 2½–3 hours, until the dough has risen and nearly reached the top of the tin. I pop the tin into the warming drawer of my oven, set on the lowest heat.

Preheat the oven to 200°C/fan 180°C/gas 6. Lightly beat the egg in a cup and brush the top of the brioche with it. Sprinkle the ginger down the centre of the loaf and scatter the top with the cinnamon sugar.

SEVILLE ORANGE BRIOCHE
Continued

Bake the brioche for 20–25 minutes, until it is a rich golden brown colour and has risen. Cool in the tin for 5 minutes, then transfer to a wire rack to cool. The loaf slices best when cold.

OVERNIGHT MUESLI WITH WARM MARMALADE HONEY PEARS

Serves 4

This is a variation on Bircher muesli, in which the oats are soaked overnight. I sometimes swap the grated apple for grated carrot. Quince and sweet orange or blood orange and vanilla marmalade are favourites for this recipe when I have some in the cupboard.

100g porridge oats
200ml milk
50g sultanas
100g hazelnuts
1 apple
150g natural yoghurt
zest of ½ an orange
zest of ½ a lemon

FOR THE PEARS
2 ripe but firm pears
3 tablespoons of your favourite marmalade
1 tablespoon runny honey
1 tablespoon each of orange and lemon juice
a small knob of butter

Preheat the oven to 180°C/fan 160°C/gas 4. In a bowl, mix the oats with the milk and sultanas, then cover and leave to soak overnight in the fridge. Roast the hazelnuts in a shallow baking tray in the oven for 7–8 minutes, until golden. Leave to cool.

OVERNIGHT MUESLI WITH WARM
MARMALADE HONEY PEARS
Continued

The next day, peel, core and quarter the pears. Put the marmalade, honey, orange and lemon juice and butter into a medium frying pan and stir together over a low heat for a few minutes. Add the pear quarters and bubble them in the mixture, turning them now and then, for 10 minutes. Meanwhile, roughly chop the hazelnuts and core and grate the apple (no need to peel it), add both to the soaked oats with the yoghurt and zest, and stir together.

Transfer the pears to a dish. Bubble the pan juices until you have about 3 tablespoons left, then spoon over the pears. Serve the warm pears with the muesli.

MARMALADE HARISSA SAUSAGES
Serves 4–6

You can never have too many variations on cocktail sausages, coated with something sticky and delicious – perfect for a party. Most bitter orange or lemon marmalades are just the ticket to use for this recipe. Seville orange with black treacle or spices and dark and moody marmalade are particularly good.

---

16 chipolatas or 24 cocktail sausages

2 tablespoons of your favourite marmalade

4 generous pinches each of ground cinnamon and ground cumin

2 teaspoons harissa

Preheat the oven to 200°C/fan 180°C/gas 6. Put the chipolatas or sausages into a small roasting tin and roast for 15–20 minutes, or until lightly golden, turning them halfway. Meanwhile, in a small bowl, mix the other ingredients, chopping any large pieces of peel in the marmalade.

After the 15–20 minutes, tip the mixture over the sausages and toss together. Roast for a further 10 minutes, basting halfway, until sticky, coated and cooked through. Eat hot.

MARMALADE-GLAZED BACON SANDWICHES

Serves 2–3

The saltiness of crisp bacon and the sweetness of marmalade work well together, a best-of-both-worlds breakfast. The only rules are, first, use white bread – this really is non-negotiable – and second, the bacon must be crisp-edged and hot enough to slightly melt the butter. Don't restrict the glazed bacon to breakfast time: grill some for longer until really crisp – it will harden as it cools and you can break it into shards to add to a chopped or leafy salad.

---

12 rashers of British smoked dry-cured streaky bacon
2 tablespoons Seville orange marmalade
a dash or two of Worcestershire sauce
soft butter
4–6 large slices of medium-sliced white bloomer bread

Preheat the grill on a high setting. Lay the rashers of bacon on a grill pan – I put them on a silicone sheet to stop them sticking. Grill the bacon for 2–3 minutes on each side, until it is part cooked. Meanwhile heat the marmalade, Worcestershire sauce and a tablespoon of water in a small pan – chop the marmalade first if it has a chunky shred (I do this with a pair of scissors when it is in the pan).

Brush one side of each bacon rasher with the marmalade glaze and return them to the grill for 3–4 minutes, until crispy on the edges. Turn the rashers and repeat.

Butter the slices of bread generously. Top with the sizzling hot, crisp bacon, sandwich together and eat while mulling over the day that lies ahead.

FLUFFY APPLE AND MARMALADE HOTCAKES WITH CINNAMON BUTTER
Makes 16

For brunch or teatime, eat these hot from the pan. I often serve them in relays for brunch when friends or family are staying for the weekend.

150g (1 small) Bramley cooking apple
100g plain flour
2 teaspoons baking powder
1 tablespoon caster sugar
3 large eggs
3 tablespoons of your favourite marmalade (apple harvest marmalade is particularly good in these)
150g ricotta
2 tablespoons milk
butter and oil, for frying

FOR THE CINNAMON BUTTER
50g soft unsalted butter
1 tablespoon marmalade
1 teaspoon cinnamon sugar

For the cinnamon butter, mix the ingredients together in a small bowl, using scissors to chop any large pieces of peel in the marmalade. Transfer the butter to the fridge to firm up.

Peel, core and dice the apple. Weigh the flour and put it into a mixing bowl, then add the baking powder, sugar and a pinch of salt and mix together. Make a well in the centre.

Crack the eggs into a small bowl, add the marmalade (again chopping any large pieces of peel), lightly whisk together with a fork, then tip into the well in the flour. Using a balloon whisk, gradually whisk the beaten eggs into the flour, followed by the ricotta and milk. Stir in the diced apple.

Heat a small knob of butter and a tablespoonful of oil in a non-stick frying pan until sizzling. Add a heaped dessertspoonful of batter per pancake, frying a few at a time over a low heat for 2–3 minutes on each side – they are ready to flip over when small bubbles appear at the edges. If the fat in the pan starts to darken and burn, wipe out the pan before heating more oil and butter.

Serve the hotcakes straight from the pan, topped with the cinnamon butter.

FLUFFY APPLE AND MARMALADE HOTCAKES WITH CINNAMON BUTTER
Continued

ALSO TRY ...

Tropical hotcakes – use lime and grapefruit or sweet orange and passion fruit marmalade in the hotcake mixture and in the flavoured butter, and substitute the cinnamon sugar with regular sugar mixed with a generous grating of nutmeg. Swap the ricotta for thick coconut yoghurt and serve the hotcakes drizzled with passion fruit pulp.

GOOEY MARMALADE, PECAN AND CARDAMOM BUNS
Makes 9

The best sticky buns I have ever had were at Balthazar restaurant in New York – they were so good I had to return the next day to try them all over again. I have made several versions over the years to try and replicate them, and this is my new favourite – it has a Scandinavian twist, with the flavour of cardamom.

150ml milk
50g butter, in small pieces
400g strong white bread flour, plus a little extra for kneading
50g light soft brown sugar
1 x 7g sachet of fast-action dried yeast
1 large egg
75g pecan halves
75 raisins (or sultanas)

FOR THE STICKY GOO
4 tablespoons of your favourite marmalade
100g light soft brown sugar
50ml double cream
50g butter

GOOEY MARMALADE, PECAN AND CARDAMOM BUNS
Continued

FOR THE CARDAMOM BUTTER

8 cardamom pods

1 teaspoon ground cinnamon

50g very soft butter

50g light soft brown sugar

50g demerara sugar

First, heat the milk in a small pan with the butter pieces until it is warm and the butter has melted, then take the pan off the heat and leave it to cool.

Tip the flour into a large bowl and stir in the sugar, yeast and half a teaspoon of salt. Lightly beat the egg in a small bowl. Make a well in the flour, then pour in the lukewarm milk (you should be able to hold your little finger in it without any discomfort) and the beaten egg.

Mix the dough initially with a large spoon, then use your hands to bring it together. Tip the dough on to a work surface and knead it for 10 minutes (you may need to dust the work surface with a little flour to start with). Alternatively, knead it in a food mixer with a dough attachment for 5 minutes. It should feel springy to the touch.

Transfer the dough to a lightly oiled bowl, cover with oiled cling film and leave it to rise in a warm place for 1½ hours, or until it has doubled in size. Meanwhile, make the sticky goo by slowly heating all the ingredients together in a small pan with a pinch of salt until melted – chop any large pieces of marmalade peel with scissors. Bubble the sauce for 2 minutes only, then leave to cool.

For the spiced butter, split the cardamom pods and remove the seeds, then mix them (lightly crush them in a pestle and mortar first if you have one) in a bowl with the cinnamon, soft butter and sugars.

Chop the nuts. Tip the risen dough out on to the work surface, punch it with your fist a couple of times to knock out the air, then knead it briefly again before pressing or gently rolling it out to a 23 x 30cm rectangle. Using a table knife, spread the spiced butter all over the dough. Evenly sprinkle the chopped nuts and the raisins on top.

Now roll up the dough as tightly as you can, like a roulade, starting from one of the shorter sides. Trim the ends and slice the roll into nine rounds, each about 2cm thick.

Pour the sticky goo into a square 20cm cake tin – not a loose-bottomed one – and arrange the buns, cut side up, in the tin in three rows of three. Leave the buns to rise again in a warm place for 45 minutes, or until doubled in size. Preheat the oven to 190°C/fan 170°C/gas 5.

GOOEY MARMALADE, PECAN AND CARDAMOM BUNS
Continued

Bake the buns for 40–45 minutes, or until risen and golden and cooked through, but cover them loosely with foil after 25 minutes to prevent them from over-browning. Don't let the foil touch the buns or it will stick.

Take the buns out of the oven, loosen around the inside of the tin with a knife, then leave the buns to cool for 20 minutes before turning them out of the tin and on to a board. Dislodge any stubborn sticky goo left in the tin and put it on top of the burnished buns. Eat warm or cold.

EASY MARMALADE AND SULTANA CUSTARD SWIRLS
Makes 16

Custardy, sweet and moreish. You can prepare these the night before you want to bake them and chill the roll overnight in the fridge.

---

1 x 320g sheet of all-butter puff pastry

25g butter

4 tablespoons marmalade, such as Seville orange, four fruit or
   lemon

125g ready-made thick custard

100g ground almonds

100g sultanas

2 tablespoons demerara sugar, plus extra to sprinkle

1 teaspoon ground mixed spice (not essential)

Take the pastry out of the fridge to allow it to soften slightly. Melt the butter and set aside to cool. In a bowl, mix the marmalade, custard, ground almonds, sultanas, the 2 tablespoons of sugar and the spice (if using) until combined.

Sprinkle a sheet of baking paper with demerara sugar and unroll the pastry on to it so that one of the longer sides is nearest to you.

EASY MARMALADE AND SULTANA CUSTARD SWIRLS
Continued

Lightly brush the pastry all over with the cooled melted butter, then spread with the filling, taking it right to the edges of the shorter sides but leaving a 2cm border along each longer side. Roll up the pastry like a Swiss roll, starting from the longer side that is nearest to you (use the paper to help you roll). Then, wrap the pastry roll in the baking paper; twist the ends and chill it in the freezer for 30 minutes.

Preheat the oven to 200°C/fan 180°C/gas 6. Slice the roll into discs at 1½–2cm intervals and arrange them flat on one or two large flat baking sheets lined with baking paper. Brush the swirls with any leftover melted butter. Bake the swirls for 15–20 minutes, or until golden. Transfer to a cooling rack using a fish slice. Eat warm or cold.

LUNCH
&
SUPPER

STICKY BARBECUED TERIYAKI QUAIL WITH CHILLED NOODLE SALAD
Serves 2

This recipe idea was born on a blisteringly hot day. As the sun went down, hunger surfaced and the barbecue was lit. Quail cook so much more quickly over the coals than chicken joints, and I defy anyone not to want to pick them up and nibble on the sticky barbecued bones.

4 quail
a small knob of root ginger
3 tablespoons light or dark soy sauce
3 tablespoons mirin
3 tablespoons marmalade such as Seville orange, lemon or lime and grapefruit

FOR THE CHILLED NOODLE SALAD
100g dried soba noodles
1 tablespoon sesame seeds
3 spring onions
2 medium carrots
1 clove of garlic
2 tablespoons groundnut oil
2 tablespoons light or dark soy sauce
1 tablespoon rice vinegar
2 tablespoons mirin
2 tablespoons salted peanuts

STICKY BARBECUED TERIYAKI QUAIL WITH CHILLED NOODLE SALAD
Continued

First you need to spatchcock the quail. This is a really easy task and it will mean they cook evenly. Put one of the quail breast-side down on a board and, using scissors, cut through either side of the backbone and lift it out. Using the flat of your hand, press firmly on the quail to flatten it. Rinse and pat dry with kitchen paper, then repeat with the rest of the quail.

For the marinade, peel the ginger and grate into a bowl, then whisk in the soy, mirin and marmalade – chop the marmalade first if it contains big pieces of peel. Lay the quail in a large shallow dish and spoon over the marinade, turn the birds in it, then cover and marinate in the fridge while you light the barbecue and make the salad.

Boil the noodles in plenty of boiling water for 5 minutes, then drain and rinse in cold water. Put them into a bowl and chill them.

Next, toast the sesame seeds in a small frying pan over a lowish heat until golden, then tip them into a bowl. Trim the spring onions and shred them. Peel the carrots and slice them into thin matchsticks. Peel and crush the garlic and mix in a small bowl with the oil, soy sauce, vinegar, mirin and sesame seeds. Toss the chilled noodles with the shredded onion, carrot and the dressing and return to the fridge until you are ready to eat, or for up to an hour. Roughly chop the peanuts and keep to one side.

Barbecue the quail over the glowing embers of the barbecue for 4–5 minutes on each side, brushing them with the marinade as they cook through and become deliciously sticky.

Toss the noodles with the peanuts and serve with the quail.

PERSIAN SPICED MEATBALLS WITH DILL YOGHURT
Serves 4

Barberries are small sour fruit that contrast well with the sweetness of marmalade. If you can't find them – Iranian shops are the place to look – use finely chopped dried sour cherries instead. I claim no grounds on authenticity here, but these vanished when I made them for a group of friends one Friday night. Serve with couscous or rice, with extra herbs and slivered pistachios stirred through.

15g dried barberries
1 tablespoon cumin seeds
1 tablespoon coriander seeds
1 clove of garlic
1 tablespoon chopped mint
2 tablespoons chopped dill
2 teaspoons sumac
1 teaspoon flaked salt
1 large egg, lightly beaten
2 tablespoons marmalade, such as Seville orange or lemon
500g lamb mince
50g fresh white breadcrumbs
1 tablespoon oil and a small knob of butter, for frying

FOR THE DILL YOGHURT

1 orange
200g authentic natural Greek yoghurt
2 tablespoons chopped pistachios
3 tablespoons chopped dill
1 teaspoon sumac

First soak the barberries in a small bowl of cold water for 15 minutes. Toast the cumin and coriander seeds in a small frying pan until they smell fragrant, which will only take a minute or so. Tip them into a pestle and mortar and crush them as finely as you can. Crush the garlic, then combine the cumin, coriander and garlic in a bowl with the mint, dill, sumac, salt and egg. Chop any large pieces of peel in the marmalade and add that too. Mix, then tip in the lamb, breadcrumbs and drained barberries and mix again thoroughly.

Form the mixture into 28 meatballs, then transfer them to the fridge to firm up for 30 minutes (longer is fine). Meanwhile, for the dill yoghurt, slice the peel from the orange, then cut out the segments and roughly chop them. Mix the chopped orange in a bowl with the other ingredients and a pinch of salt.

Heat the oil and butter in a frying pan. Fry the meatballs for 8–10 minutes over a medium heat until cooked through, turning them from time to time so they become golden all over. Serve with the dill yoghurt.

VIETNAMESE STYLE CARAMEL PORK WITH A CUCUMBER AND PEANUT SALAD
Serves 4

Serve with rice. The sauce and salad also partner well with roast rump of lamb or crispy lamb cutlets.

1.2kg piece of boneless pork belly
2 teaspoons crushed flaky sea salt

FOR THE SAUCE
2 bird-eye chillies
75ml rice vinegar
1 tablespoon Thai fish sauce
2 tablespoons marmalade, such as lemon or lime
   and grapefruit
100g caster sugar
the juice of 1 lime

FOR THE SALAD
3 tablespoons rice vinegar
1 teaspoon Thai fish sauce
2 teaspoons sugar
2 tablespoons shredded mint leaves
2 tablespoons chopped coriander leaves
1 cucumber
3 medium carrots
3 tablespoons chopped roasted peanuts

Preheat the oven to 200°C/fan 180°C/gas 6. Put the pork belly on a rack in a roasting tin, sprinkle the skin with the salt and roast the meat for 30 minutes. Then reduce the oven temperature to 180°C/fan 160°C/gas 4 and continue cooking the pork for a further 1½ hours, until the skin has turned to golden crackling.

For the caramel sauce, deseed and finely chop the chillies and put them into a measuring jug with the vinegar, fish sauce and marmalade (chopped first if it contains large pieces of peel). Scatter the sugar in an even layer in a small pan or frying pan over a low heat until it has melted and turned to a dark amber caramel. You want all the sugar granules to melt and turn to a rich golden caramel – once most of the sugar granules have melted, give the caramel a stir from time to time and keep an eye on it, as the colour turns quickly. As soon as it is a rich golden colour, take the pan off the heat and pour in the vinegar mixture (be careful, as it may spit), stirring. Return to a low heat and keep stirring until the sauce has come back together again. Don't panic if there are sugary lumps. Just be patient, they will re-melt over a low heat. Pour it into a heatproof jug, stir in the lime juice and leave to cool.

Next, put the vinegar, Thai fish sauce, sugar, herbs and a pinch of salt into a large bowl and toss together. Using a flat-bladed peeler, slice the cucumber and carrot into lengths and toss with the vinegar mixture in the bowl, then leave to one side.

Serve the pork cut into squares, with some of the sauce drizzled on top. Add the peanuts to the salad and serve alongside the pork. Pour the rest of the sauce into a bowl to put on the table.

ROAST CHICKEN WITH PERRY, APPLES AND KUMQUATS
Serves 4

Perry, for those who haven't come across it before, is an English alcoholic pear drink, usually called pear cider. Serve this main course with a hearty root mash – I like a mix of parsnip, celeriac and carrot – and salad or buttered leafy spring greens.

2 large red onions
2 apples
200g kumquats
butter and oil, for frying
2 tablespoons chopped thyme leaves, plus a few sprigs
4 part-boned skin-on chicken breasts
1 fat clove of garlic
8 juniper berries
1–2 tablespoons Seville orange or lemon marmalade
500ml vintage English perry
75–100g sliced pancetta
200ml crème fraîche

Peel the red onions, halve them, then slice each half into wedges through the root. Quarter and core the apples, then slice each quarter in half lengthways. Halve the kumquats lengthways.

Heat a knob of butter and a tablespoon of oil in a frying pan until it sizzles, then brown the onions and transfer them to a roasting tin as they are ready. Next, brown the apple wedges and add them to the tin with the thyme sprigs.

Preheat the oven to 200°C/fan 180°C/gas 6. Add a little more butter and oil to the pan and when sizzling, brown the chicken breasts for 8–10 minutes, turning them from time to time, until they are gloriously golden all over. Meanwhile, peel and crush the garlic and smash the juniper berries in a pestle and mortar to split them.

Put the chicken on top of the apples and onions and season with crushed sea salt and pepper. Wipe out the frying pan, add another small knob of butter, and fry the garlic for 30 seconds before adding the marmalade, chopped thyme, juniper berries and perry. Bring to a simmer and bubble together for a minute, then pour over the chicken. Lay the sliced pancetta on the chicken breasts and scatter the kumquats in the tin. Roast everything for 30 minutes.

Transfer the onions, apples and chicken to a serving platter and keep warm. Bubble the cooking juices in the tin on the hob, stirring in the crème fraîche and seasoning to taste. Spoon some of the sauce on top of the chicken and pour the rest into a warm jug to hand round.

JOSÉ PIZARRO'S GRIDDLED PRAWNS WITH CAULIFLOWER PURÉE AND CORIANDER

Serves 2, or 4 as a starter

José Pizarro's welcoming restaurants in south-east London are two of my favourite haunts, and he has taught me a lot about Spanish food. If you want to make this lovely recipe with freshly squeezed sweet orange juice, add a squeeze of lemon too so the sauce isn't too sweet. Make the purée when you marinate the prawns if you want to get ahead of the game, and just reheat it to serve.

8–12 large unpeeled raw juicy prawns

juice of 2–3 Seville (or sweet, see above) oranges – you need 75ml juice

2 tablespoons chopped marmalade, Seville orange or lemon

a generous pinch of crushed dried chillies

1 whole small cauliflower (600–700g)

500ml milk

olive oil, for brushing

2–3 tablespoons chopped coriander

2–3 tablespoons chopped toasted blanched almonds or flaked almonds

---

Peel and devein the prawns but keep the tails intact. In a shallow bowl, mix the orange juice, marmalade and chilli; add the prawns and turn them in the juice, then leave to marinate in the fridge for a couple of hours, giving them a turn now and then.

A Pot of Marmalade

Remove the leaves and tough stalk from the cauliflower and break the curds into florets, then put them into a medium pan with a pinch of salt. Add the milk and 300ml of water and bring to simmering point, then put a lid on the pan, reduce the heat to low, and simmer for 15–20 minutes, or until the cauliflower is tender. Drain thoroughly, then put into a food processor and whiz to a purée, seasoning with salt and freshly ground black pepper. Keep warm in a low oven.

Preheat a griddle over a high heat. Take the prawns out of their marinade, then brush the griddle with oil and cook the prawns on it for 2–3 minutes on each side, until cooked through and lightly charred. At the same time tip the marinade into a frying pan or wide-based pan and bubble it over a high heat to reduce it. Stir in the coriander.

Sprinkle a little salt on the cooked prawns. Divide the cauliflower purée between two or four warmed plates, top with the prawns, drizzle with the sauce and scatter over the nuts.

WARM BULGAR WHEAT AND WATERCRESS SALAD WITH GOAT'S CURD AND CITRUS DRESSING Serves 4–6

The soft texture of goat's curd works well with the nutty wheat, crunchy almonds and wake-me-up dressing. Seville orange juice is tart and the zest fragrant, so, if the oranges are in season when you make this, make the most of their flavour and use them instead of lemon.

200g bulgar wheat
50g skin-on almonds (or toasted blanched almonds)
100g watercress
zest and juice of 1 lemon or Seville orange
2 tablespoons olive oil
3 tablespoons marmalade, such as lemon or Seville orange
125g tenderstem broccoli tips
1 x 400g tin of chickpeas
2–3 tablespoons shredded mint
150g goat's curd or soft goat's cheese

Tip the bulgar wheat into a pan and add 500ml of cold water. Bring to the boil, then reduce the heat and simmer, partially covered, for 15 minutes, until tender – most of the water will be absorbed during cooking.

Meanwhile, roughly chop the almonds and remove any tough stalks from the watercress. Put the watercress into a mixing bowl, breaking up any large sprigs.

In a small bowl, mix the lemon or orange zest and juice with the olive oil, marmalade and some seasoning. Cook the broccoli in boiling salted water for 3–4 minutes, until just tender. Add half the dressing to the watercress and toss together.

If necessary, drain the cooked bulgar wheat, then tip it back into the pan and mix with the drained chickpeas and the mint; season well.

Arrange half the watercress in a bowl and spoon over half the bulgar wheat, then add half the broccoli, almonds and goat's curd or goat's cheese – add this in spoonfuls or small pieces. Repeat with the rest of the ingredients and drizzle with the remaining dressing, then tuck in.

JERK-SEASONED SLOW-ROAST SHOULDER OF PORK WITH PINEAPPLE
Serves 6–8

This has all the delicious flavour that you find in jerk seasoning, except this recipe is aromatic rather than highly spiced – it was inspired by the food we ate, flip-flop clad with the beating sun on our backs, from the roadside stalls in the Cayman Islands, happy days!

400g shallots, regular or echalion

2 garlic cloves

2 bay leaves

1 boneless shoulder of pork, about 2.8kg

3 teaspoons crushed flaky sea salt

3 teaspoons ground allspice

1 teaspoon freshly ground black pepper

1 teaspoon ground cinnamon

2 tablespoons chopped thyme leaves

1 tablespoon oil

400ml white wine

4 tablespoons Seville orange marmalade

6 tablespoons diced pineapple

juice of a lime

2 tablespoons chopped coriander

Preheat the oven to 220°C/fan 200°C/gas 7.

Peel the shallots, halve them and use them to make a bed for the pork in a roasting tin. Peel and halve the garlic cloves and scatter on top of the shallots with the bay leaves.

Score the skin of the pork. I use a Stanley knife for this job. Mix two teaspoons of the salt and allspice with the pepper, cinnamon, chopped thyme and oil to make a paste and rub it all over the underside of the meat.

Put the pork on top of the bed of shallots. Mix together the remaining teaspoon of salt and allspice and rub into the pork skin.

In a jug, mix the wine with the marmalade and pour into the tin. Roast the pork for 30 minutes. Then, reduce the oven temperature to 160°C/fan 140°C/gas 3. Cover the tin with foil and return the pork to the oven to cook slowly for 4 hours.

In a bowl, mix the pineapple with the lime juice and coriander.

Take the pork out of the oven and increase the oven temperature again to 200°C/fan 180°C/gas 6. Remove the skin from the joint and transfer it to a baking tray, then return to the hot oven for 25–30 minutes to crisp up. Cover the pork with foil, on a carving board.

JERK-SEASONED SLOW-ROAST SHOULDER OF PORK WITH PINEAPPLE
Continued

Tip the contents of the tin into a large measuring jug and allow the fat to settle on top so you can skim it off. Then, put the roasting tin over direct heat and return the shallots and cooking juices to it. Bubble the juices for a few minutes – you can fish out the bay leaves and discard them.

Carve the pork and break up the crackling. Arrange the pork on a platter and spoon over some of the hot shallots and juices from the roasting tin. Sprinkle with the pineapple. Put the crackling in a bowl, pour the rest of the roasting tin sauce into a jug, and hand round both at the table for everyone to add as they eat.

STICKY CARROTS WITH CIDER VINEGAR AND BAY

Serves 4

A recipe for spring when bunched carrots are a-plenty. Serve as part of a vegetable mezze, or with lamb or pork.

1 x 400g bunch of slender carrots (about 8)
1 tablespoon marmalade, such as Seville orange, lemon or apple harvest
1 tablespoon cider vinegar or white wine vinegar
1 tablespoon groundnut or rapeseed oil
a couple of bay leaves

Preheat the oven to 200°C/fan180°C/gas 6. Trim the carrots and scrub them. Quarter or halve them lengthways, depending on their size.

Put the carrots into a pan and pour in enough boiling water to just cover them. Add a pinch of salt, bring back to the boil, then cook the carrots for 5 minutes and drain. While they are cooking, chop the marmalade with scissors into a mixing bowl, then stir in the vinegar and oil.

Drain the carrots and put them into the bowl. Add the bay leaves and toss together, then tip everything on to a medium baking tray. Roast for 20–25 minutes, turning halfway, until sticky and cooked through.

SHOULDER OF LAMB WITH QUINCE, IRANIAN LIME AND A BROAD BEAN AND PINE NUT PILAF

Serves 6

Sometimes you want a recipe that involves little preparation but is fit for a gathering. This is easy to throw together, leaving the oven to do most of the work, and it has become one of our top ten Sunday lunches at home. The Iranian lime adds a sharpness which is just the thing with the sweetness of the marmalade and prunes – I buy it in small jars from ottolenghi.co.uk.

6 cloves of garlic

2 or 3 large quince (900g)

1 shoulder of lamb, weighing 1.6kg

a knob of butter and oil, for frying

150ml fruity white wine

200ml hot vegetable stock

½ teaspoon ground turmeric

1 tablespoon ground Iranian lime

a pinch of saffron

3 tablespoons marmalade (I favour lemon for this recipe)

1 tablespoon runny honey

200g soft Agen prunes (optional)

FOR THE PILAF

200g double podded broad beans, frozen and defrosted are fine

1 tablespoon oil

1 tablespoon cumin seeds

100g pine nuts

250g basmati rice
500ml hot vegetable stock.
250g young leaf spinach

Preheat the oven to 160°C/fan 140°C/gas 3. Peel the garlic cloves and halve them lengthways. Peel, core and quarter the quince lengthways, then halve each quarter.

Put the lamb into a large roasting tin (or large flameproof casserole). Season with sea salt and pepper, rubbing the seasoning into the meat. Heat a knob of butter and a tablespoon of oil in a frying pan and brown the garlic, scattering it around the lamb as it is ready. Fry the quince for a few minutes on each side too and add to the tin along with any buttery juices from the pan.

Mix the wine and hot vegetable stock in a jug with the turmeric, Iranian lime, saffron, marmalade and honey and pour over the meat and fruit.

Bring everything to the boil on the hob, then cover the tin with a tent of kitchen foil (or a lid) and transfer the lamb to the oven for 2½ hours, basting the meat from time to time.

At the end of this time, scatter the prunes around the lamb, if using. Either way, cook the lamb for a further hour.

SHOULDER OF LAMB WITH QUINCE, IRANIAN LIME AND A BROAD BEAN AND PINE NUT PILAF
Continued

For the pilaf, first slip the broad beans out of their skins. Next, heat the oil in a sauté pan and toast the cumin seeds and pine nuts, stirring them together over the heat for a minute or two. Tip in the rice and add a generous pinch of salt. Stir once, then add the stock. Bring to a simmer, cover with a lid and leave to cook for 10 minutes. Scatter the broad beans on top and cook for a further 5 minutes, or until the rice is tender.

Transfer the lamb to a carving board and shred it. Put the lamb, garlic, quince and prunes on a platter and keep warm.

Tip the cooking juices into a measuring jug and skim off the fat which will rise to the surface. Return the cooking juices to the tin and bubble them on the hob for a few minutes, seasoning to taste.

Add the spinach to the pilaf in handfuls, stirring to wilt it. Drizzle the cooking juices over the meat and serve with the pilaf.

MANCHEGO FRITTERS WITH CHICORY, ORANGE AND OLIVES AND A SEVILLE ORANGE DRESSING
Serves 4

On a recent trip to Seville we ate deliciously thin, crisp prawn fritters at one of our favourite bustling tapas bars, which sparked the idea for this recipe – these cheesy fritters are very moreish. Use reserva sherry vinegar for the dressing if you can – it is aged for at least two years and has a rounder flavour than the bog-standard vinegar.

2 tablespoons pine nuts
2 oranges
12 pitted green olives
2 heads of white or red chicory
a small handful of flat-leaf parsley leaves

FOR THE FRITTERS
2 spring onions
1 tablespoon light olive oil, plus extra for frying
150g chickpea (gram) flour
½ teaspoon baking powder
¼ teaspoon smoked paprika, plus extra for sprinkling
3 tablespoons finely grated Manchego cheese
1 tablespoon finely chopped flat-leaf parsley

Continued

FOR DRESSING

1 small clove of garlic

1½ tablespoon reserva sherry vinegar

3 tablespoons olive oil

3 tablespoons marmalade, such as Seville orange or lemon

Toast the pine nuts in a sauté pan for 3–4 minutes, until golden, giving them a shake from time to time, then tip them on to a plate and set aside. Roughly chop the spring onions for the fritters, then soften them in the sauté pan in the tablespoon of olive oil and transfer them to a mixing bowl to cool.

For the dressing, peel and crush the garlic, then whiz all the ingredients in a blender with a pinch of salt.

Tip the chickpea flour into the bowl to join the onions, along with the baking powder, smoked paprika and half a teaspoon of salt. Stir, then add 200ml of cold water and mix to form a batter. Stir in the grated cheese and the chopped parsley.

Peel and slice the oranges, adding any juice to the dressing. Slice the olives too. Separate the chicory leaves and toss them in a bowl with half the salad dressing, then divide between four plates with the orange slices, olives, parsley leaves and pine nuts. Preheat the oven on a low setting – 140°C/fan 120°C/gas 1 – so you can keep the cooked fritters warm.

Heat 2cm of oil in the sauté pan. When it is smoking, turn down the heat and fry the fritters, using about a tablespoon of batter for each one; the batter should be thin enough that you can spread it out to 5–6cm with the back of the spoon once it hits the hot oil. If it seems a little too thick, add a touch more water to the batter.

Fry a couple of fritters at a time for 2 minutes on each side, or until golden. As they are ready, remove them with a fish slice to a plate lined with kitchen paper and keep warm in the low oven while you fry the rest. You should make 12 in total.

Drizzle the salad with more dressing. Sprinkle the warm fritters with salt and a little smoked paprika and divide between the plates.

CHRISTMAS HAM WITH CRANBERRIES AND SLOE GIN
Serves 10–12

Check with your butcher whether the ham you buy needs soaking overnight before you start, though with modern cures this is increasingly unnecessary. If I am making this for a party or at Christmas time, I slice a couple of clementines or limes, arrange them in a single layer on a baking sheet and grill them for a few minutes until charred at the edges. Then, once cooled, I lay them on top of the glazed fat, pushing a few extra cloves through the centre of each slice to secure them.

1 x 2kg ham, smoked or unsmoked
1 carrot
1 onion, peeled and studded with a few cloves
a few peppercorns
2 bay leaves
a few sprigs of thyme
500ml cider

FOR THE GLAZE
3–4 tablespoons marmalade (try Seville orange, lemon or kumquat and cranberry)
1 tablespoon English mustard
100g demerara sugar
about 40 cloves

FOR THE SAUCE

6 tablespoons marmalade (see above)

450g fresh cranberries

4 tablespoons sloe gin (or port)

1 tablespoon English mustard

juice of 1 clementine or lime

Preheat the oven to 160°C/fan 140°C/gas 3. Put the ham in a large roasting tin. Chop the carrot and scatter in the tin. Add the onion, peppercorns, bay leaves and thyme and pour in the cider. Cover the tin loosely with foil and bake the ham for 2 hours 45 minutes, turning it halfway through. Leave the ham until it is cool enough to handle.

Preheat the oven to 220°C/fan 200°C/gas 7. Put the glaze ingredients into a small bowl and mix to combine. For the sauce, bubble the ingredients together in a saucepan for 5 minutes, until the cranberries are starting to burst. Tip into a bowl and set aside.

Transfer the cooled ham to a baking tray and stand it upright. You don't need the ham stock for this recipe, but taste it – if it isn't too salty, strain it and freeze it to use in soups. Remove the skin of the ham using a small, sharp knife, making sure you leave the thick layer of fat intact underneath. Score the fat in a diamond pattern with criss-cross cuts.

CHRISTMAS HAM WITH CRANBERRIES AND SLOE GIN
Continued

Spread the glaze all over the fat and put the ham back into the oven for 20–25 minutes, basting now and then until the glaze is sticky. Serve warm or cold, with the cranberry sauce.

SUGAR-CURED DUCK WITH PLUMS, ORANGE AND MARSALA
Serves 4

Making a brine for the duck keeps it extra juicy when roasted and tender to eat. I serve this with some buttery mashed celeriac on the side.

25g rock salt
40g caster sugar
a few black peppercorns
a couple of sprigs of rosemary
2 cloves of garlic
4 duck legs, 175–200g each
6–8 plums

FOR THE SAUCE
2 shallots
50g cold butter
250ml freshly squeezed orange juice
100ml chicken stock
1 bay leaf
2 tablespoons marmalade (I like the bitterness of Seville
    orange or lemon)
3 tablespoons Marsala
a squeeze of lemon juice

SUGAR-CURED DUCK WITH PLUMS, ORANGE AND MARSALA
Continued

Put the salt, sugar, peppercorns and rosemary into a pan and pour in 1 litre of water. Squash the unpeeled garlic cloves with the flat side of a knife so they split, and add to the pan. Bring the liquid to simmering point, then turn off the heat and leave it to cool completely.

Tip the cold brine into a plastic box, bowl or dish. Add the duck legs – they should be fully immersed. Cover and chill overnight, or just for a couple of hours if you want to cook the duck the same day.

Preheat the oven to 180°C/fan 160°C/gas 4. Remove the duck legs from the brine, which can now be discarded, and pat them dry with kitchen paper. Put the duck legs into a roasting tin and prick the skin all over. Roast the duck for 1 hour 30 minutes, adding the plums, stoned and quartered, for the final 30 minutes.

For the sauce, peel and finely chop the shallots. Melt a little of the butter in a pan and gently cook the shallots until really soft. Add the orange juice, stock and bay leaf, then bring to the boil and bubble to reduce by half. Cube the remaining butter.

Stir the marmalade, Marsala and a squeeze of lemon juice into the sauce and bubble for a further minute, then whisk in the cubed butter and take the pan off the heat.

Put the crispy duck legs on a platter, scatter the plums around them and drizzle some of the sauce over the top. Serve the rest of the sauce alongside.

PUDDINGS

TOAST AND MARMALADE TART
Serves 8–12

Toasting the breadcrumbs gives an added depth of flavour to this tart, which is a good make-ahead pud – bake the whole tart a few hours before you want to eat it, or bake the pastry case, cool it, and fill it just before baking to serve warm. Either way, serve with generous scoops of clotted cream or vanilla ice cream.

350g shortcrust pastry
150g fresh white breadcrumbs
1 x 454g tin of golden syrup
3 tablespoons marmalade, Seville orange or lemon
a pinch of ground ginger
zest and juice of 1 large lemon
2 large eggs
75ml double cream

Preheat the oven to 200°C/fan 180°C/gas 6. Line a 23cm round and 4.5cm deep fluted tin with the pastry and chill for 20 minutes.

Scatter the breadcrumbs on a baking tray and toast in the oven for 10–12 minutes, until nicely golden, turning them halfway with a spoon. Leave to cool.

Line the chilled pastry shell with a circle of baking paper (scrunch it up and open it out again so it fits nicely) and some ceramic baking beans (uncooked rice works well too). Bake the pastry

---

TOAST AND MARMALADE TART
Continued

---

shell, on a baking tray, for 20 minutes, then take the paper and
beans out and bake for a further 10 minutes, until lightly golden.

Meanwhile, tip the syrup into a pan and stir in the marmalade and
ginger. Heat gently until warm.

Put the lemon zest and juice into a bowl and pour on the warm
syrupy mixture. Lightly beat the eggs, then stir them in too, along
with the cream and the toasted breadcrumbs, and give everything
a thorough mix to combine.

As soon as the pastry shell is ready, take it out of the oven and
reduce the oven temperature to 180°C/fan 160°C/gas 4. Tip the
filling mixture into the pastry case and bake it for 30 minutes.

Serve warm or cold – sliced into eight or twelve, let your own
sweet tooth be your guide.

MARMALADE, GINGER AND SEVILLE ORANGE ICE CREAM
Serves 6–8

I'm not a fan of unnecessary kitchen gadgetry but I wouldn't be without my ice cream maker. It saves endless whisking and the risk of ice crystals – it still fascinates me how it turns my mixtures into ready-to-scoop ice cream in so little time; it's kitchen magic. But I have also given instructions for making this ice cream by hand, which works well too. If Seville oranges aren't in season, omit the juice.

400ml whole milk
150ml double cream
1 cinnamon stick
2 balls of stem ginger in syrup
juice of 2–3 bitter Seville oranges (you need 75ml juice)
4 large egg yolks
75g golden caster sugar
1 teaspoon cornflour
4 tablespoons Seville orange marmalade (the tonka bean
    variety is perfect for this recipe) or lemon marmalade

Pour the milk and cream into a medium pan and add the cinnamon stick. Stir together, then slowly bring to the boil and turn off the heat. Meanwhile (but keeping an eye on the pan, as the milk easily boils over), drain the balls of ginger and chop into small pieces, and squeeze the oranges.

MARMALADE, GINGER AND SEVILLE ORANGE ICE CREAM
Continued

Put the egg yolks and sugar into a bowl and whisk thoroughly to combine – I use a balloon whisk. Mix in the cornflour, then pour in the hot milk (fish out the cinnamon stick), whisking all the time.

Return the whole lot to the (rinsed out) pan and stir over a low heat until thickened. Don't let it come to the boil – the custard is ready when it coats the back of a wooden spoon but you need to be patient.

When the custard is ready, tip it into a bowl and stir in the chopped ginger, marmalade and orange juice. Leave the ice cream mixture to cool completely (put it over a bowl of ice if you have some), giving it a stir from time to time.

Churn the mixture in an ice cream maker according to the manufacturer's instructions. Alternatively, freeze in a plastic container for a couple of hours until it is starting to firm up around the edges, then whisk with an electric hand whisk, freeze for a further 2–3 hours, repeat, then freeze until solid.

A QUICK MARMALADE SAUCE
Serves 4

This takes minutes to make and is so versatile. Use your favourite marmalade, adding whichever alcohol fits flavour-wise. Seville double orange or ginger and rum, four fruit and pink grapefruit are four I would choose to use. You can add chopped toasted nuts, or a handful of raisins might tick the box if you make the sauce with rum. Serve over vanilla ice cream, pancakes or poached fruit, with some Greek yoghurt on the side.

---

1 tablespoon butter

3 tablespoons of your favourite marmalade

2 oranges

1 lemon

1 tablespoon dark muscovado sugar

2 tablespoons Cointreau, Grand Marnier, whisky or dark rum

1 teaspoon arrowroot

First, melt the butter in a small pan until gently sizzling. Add the marmalade and stir together over the heat for a minute or so. Meanwhile juice the oranges and the lemon.

A QUICK MARMALADE SAUCE
Continued

Add the juice, the sugar and the booze to the pan and bubble
everything together for a few minutes. Meanwhile, put the
arrowroot into a small cup, add a teaspoonful of cold water and
mix. Add a tablespoon of the hot sauce, mix and stir back into the
pan. Bubble together briefly, then pour the sauce into a jug. I like
to serve it lukewarm.

HOT CHOCOLATE FONDANTS WITH BITTER ORANGE MIDDLES
Serves 6

Chocoholics' delight! These fondant puddings have rich, melting, chocolatey centres and you can assemble them a couple of hours before baking them; they've never let me down.

150g unsalted butter
200g dark chocolate (around 70% cocoa solids)
2 medium eggs
2 medium egg yolks
125g golden caster sugar
50g plain flour
4 tablespoons Seville orange marmalade – use the double
    orange or tonka bean marmalade if you have made them
2 tablespoons chilled crème fraîche, plus extra to serve

Cut the butter into small pieces, then melt it with the chocolate (I do this in a bowl over a pan of barely simmering water); leave to cool for 10 minutes. Preheat the oven to 200°C/fan 180°C/gas 6 and preheat a baking tray at the same time. Grease six 150ml non-stick mini pudding basins.

In a mixing bowl and using an electric hand whisk, whisk the eggs, yolks and sugar together for 5 minutes until light and airy. Finally, whisk in the flour and the melted chocolate and butter.

HOT CHOCOLATE FONDANTS WITH BITTER ORANGE MIDDLES
Continued

Add some chocolate mixture to each mini pudding basin so they are nearly half full. Chop the marmalade in a cup, using scissors. Mix the marmalade with the chilled crème fraîche and add some to each pudding – make a slight dip in the centre of the chocolate mixture to spoon it on to. Top with the remaining chocolate mixture, spreading it out as best you can; it doesn't need to be neat and perfect. The amount of mixture in the pudding basins might look a little mean, but they will rise to perfection in the oven.

Put the puddings on the hot baking tray and bake them for 12 minutes – make sure you set a timer. Leave them to settle, out of the oven, for 5 minutes, then carefully run a knife around the inside of each one and turn them out. Serve with extra crème fraîche.

QUEEN OF PUDDINGS WITH A TWIST

Serves 6

A nursery pud favourite – warm citrus custard topped with billowing meringue. You can bake the base a few hours ahead. Serve with chilled pouring cream.

100g white breadcrumbs

300ml double cream

200ml whole milk

50g butter

2 tablespoons dark rum

3 large eggs

125g caster sugar

finely grated zest of 1 lime (or lemon)

3 tablespoons lime and grapefruit or lemon marmalade

Butter a 1.5 litre ovenproof dish measuring about 21cm by 9cm deep and scatter the breadcrumbs in the bottom of the dish.

Heat the cream and milk in a pan with the butter and rum until the butter has melted, stir, then cool until just warm.

Separate the eggs – the yolks into a medium bowl and the whites into a big bowl. Whisk the yolks with 50g of the sugar to combine, then whisk in the warm cream and milk. Pour this over the breadcrumbs, stir, and leave to soak for 20 minutes. Preheat the oven to 180°C/fan 160°C/gas 4.

QUEEN OF PUDDINGS WITH A TWIST
Continued

Bake the pudding base for 30 minutes.

Mix the lime zest with the marmalade and add in teaspoonfuls to the top of the hot baked custard. Whisk the egg whites until stiff, then gradually add the remaining 75g of sugar and keep whisking until you have a glossy meringue. Spoon on top of the custard base.

Finally, bake the pudding for 15–20 minutes until the meringue is risen and tinged golden. Eat warm.

MINI LEMON AND BLACKCURRANT PUDDINGS

Serves 4

I first made these when I needed a quick pud and had some blackcurrants in the freezer; adding the blackcurrants to the mixture while still frozen means they keep their shape when baked. Serve with scoops of vanilla ice cream.

---

4 tablespoons lemon marmalade

75g soft butter, plus extra for greasing

75g plain flour

2 teaspoons baking powder

2 medium eggs

75g light muscovado sugar

100g frozen blackcurrants

Preheat the oven to 180°C/fan 160°C/gas 4. Generously butter four 150ml non-stick mini pudding basins and line each base with a circle of non-stick baking paper; butter those too. Divide the marmalade between the basins – loosen it with 1–2 teaspoons of boiling water first, depending on how firm it is.

In a mixing bowl, whisk together the butter, flour, baking powder, eggs and sugar until smooth. Gently fold in the frozen black-currants and divide the mixture between the four basins; place them on a large baking tray.

MINI LEMON AND BLACKCURRANT PUDDINGS
Continued

Bake the puddings for 20 minutes, or until golden and risen. Once out of the oven, set them aside for 5 minutes to settle, then run a knife around the inside edge of each basin and turn the puddings out on to plates. Remove the base papers and serve.

CASSATA CHEESECAKE
Serves 12

Cassata siciliana, a sweet ricotta cake, is an elaborate, classic Sicilian dessert and this cheesecake has similar ingredients; the marmalade replaces the traditional candied peel. Serve with small glasses of chilled Marsala and a jug of cream.

75g plain flour
275g golden caster sugar
40g soft butter
3 large eggs
100g pistachio nuts
100g dark chocolate (around 70% cocoa solids)
2 x 60g packs dried cherries
2 x 280g tubs full-fat cream cheese, at room temperature
250g ricotta, at room temperature
150ml double cream
3 tablespoons marmalade – lemon or pink grapefruit are good
    choices
2 tablespoons Marsala
1 heaped tablespoon cornflour
icing sugar, for dusting

Preheat the oven to 190°C/fan 170°C/gas 5. Put the flour, 75g of the sugar and the butter into a food processor and whiz to fine crumbs (or rub the butter into the flour by hand and then stir in the sugar), then press into the base and roughly halfway up the

---

CASSATA CHEESECAKE
Continued

---

sides of a well-buttered 22–23cm springform tin – it will be a very thin layer, but that is how it should be. Put the tin on a baking tray.

Lightly beat the eggs with a fork in a small bowl. Roughly chop the pistachios, chocolate and cherries – you may find scissors are the easiest way to chop up the cherries. Now, in a mixing bowl, whisk together the rest of the sugar, the eggs, cream cheese, ricotta, cream, marmalade, Marsala and cornflour. Stir in the chopped pistachios, chocolate and cherries.

Transfer the cheesecake mixture to the tin. The mixture will pretty much fill the tin. Bake the cheesecake for 1 hour 15 minutes, covering it with foil after 45 minutes to prevent over-browning. Turn off the heat, but leave the cheesecake to cool in the oven with the door ajar.

When cold, remove the cheesecake from the tin and transfer to a serving plate. Serve slightly chilled and generously dusted with icing sugar.

15-MINUTE LEMON PASSION FRUIT POTS
Serves 8

The easiest pud ever. You can make the passion fruit and lemon syrup well in advance, leaving you to just whip the cream when it suits.

---

2 large passion fruit

zest and juice of 2 lemons

2 tablespoons marmalade, such as lemon, sweet orange and passion fruit or lemon and limoncello

2 tablespoons caster sugar

4 tablespoons limoncello

300ml double cream, chilled

crystallised violets or rose petals (I buy these from janeasher.com)

Halve the passion fruit and scoop the flesh into a sieve set over a bowl. Sieve the flesh so you end up with the orangey-coloured juice in the bowl, pressing the flesh in the sieve with the back of a spoon to make sure you get every last bit. Discard the passion fruit seeds.

Add the lemon zest and juice, the marmalade, sugar and limoncello to the bowl. Stir to dissolve.

In another bowl, whisk the chilled cream until it forms soft peaks, then add the lemon mixture, little by little, still whisking. Spoon into small glasses. You can chill the pots at this stage if you're not serving them straight away. Top with crystallised violets or rose petals to serve.

ANNA DEL CONTE'S MARMALADE AND APPLE CROSTATA

Serves 8

'Anna, do you have a favourite Italian recipe that uses marmalade?' I asked. 'No,' she replied with conviction, then luckily remembered this recipe. 'How silly of me, I just remembered that I used to make a good marmalade tart – just add lemon zest to my sweet pastry and sprinkle the base with blanched ground almonds. But, grind them yourself,' she warned. 'The bought sort are too fine.' So I did, and here is the recipe with the addition of some grated apple. The sweet and crunchy pastry recipe is based on the version in Anna's book *Gastronomy of Italy*, a must-have for anyone serious about Italian food.

250g Italian '00' flour (or strong white bread flour), plus a little
    extra for rolling out
100g icing sugar
grated zest of ½ a lemon
150g unsalted butter, at room temperature
1 large egg
1 large egg yolk

FOR THE FILLING
100g blanched almonds
1 tart eating apple (about 175g)
about 8 heaped tablespoons of your favourite marmalade –
    I like to use quince and sweet orange, sweet orange and
    passion fruit or blood orange and vanilla
grated zest of ½ a lemon
a little beaten egg, for brushing

ANNA DEL CONTE'S MARMALADE AND APPLE CROSTATA
Continued

Tip the flour into a mixing bowl, sift the icing sugar on top and sprinkle over the zest of half a lemon; mix together. Cut the butter into pieces and add it to the bowl, then, using your fingertips, rub the butter lightly into the flour and icing sugar.

Lightly beat the egg and yolk, with a fork, in a small bowl to combine, then add them to the mix. At first, use a palette knife to blend the ingredients, then bring the dough together with your hands, kneading it as little as possible.

Flatten the pastry into a disc and wrap it in cling film, then chill for 30 minutes or longer. Anna says if you make the pastry a day ahead, it will be more crumbly when cooked, but do bring it to room temperature before attempting to roll it out.

For the filling, whiz the almonds in a food processor or liquidiser until they are coarsely and evenly ground. On a lightly floured work surface, roll out two-thirds of the pastry and use it to line a 23cm fluted tart tin 3–4cm deep, trimming the edges to fit and keeping any trimmings. Sprinkle the coarsely ground almonds over the base, distributing them as evenly as possible. Peel, core and coarsely grate the apple. Mix the marmalade with the lemon zest and grated apple, then add it in spoonfuls to the tart and spread it out.

Brush the edges of the pastry with beaten egg. Combine the remaining third of the pastry with the trimmings and roll them out into a rectangle, about 25cm long. Cut out six 2cm strips to twist and lay over the top of the marmalade. Then cut out a further six to arrange in the opposite direction, to make a lattice. Brush the twisted strips with beaten egg. Chill the tart for a further 20 minutes.

Preheat the oven to 200°C/fan 180°C/gas 6 and preheat a baking tray at the same time.

Bake the tart on the preheated baking tray for 35–40 minutes, until gloriously golden. Take it out of the oven and leave for 20 minutes before removing from the tin to serve, or cool the tart completely in the tin if you want to serve it cold.

COCONUT, PAPAYA AND GRAPEFRUIT MERINGUE ROULADE

Serves 8

I buy small packs of ready-prepared coconut chunks for this recipe and grate them in a food processor or by hand. You can make and bake the roulade a few hours ahead, but once it is filled, it must be eaten with haste.

4 large egg whites
225g caster sugar
1 teaspoon cornflour
2 tablespoons grated fresh coconut, plus extra to finish
2 tablespoons icing sugar, plus extra for dusting
1 ripe papaya
1 teaspoon lemon juice
300g authentic natural Greek yoghurt
3 tablespoons lime and grapefruit or pink grapefruit
   marmalade

Preheat the oven to 180°C/fan 160°C/gas 4 and line a 20 x 30cm Swiss roll tin with non-stick baking paper.

Whisk the egg whites in a large clean bowl until they form stiff peaks, then gradually add the caster sugar, little by little, whisking all the time and adding the cornflour and the 2 tablespoons of grated coconut with the final addition of sugar.

Gently pile the meringue mix into the tin and spread it out with a palette knife. Bake for 5 minutes, then reduce the oven temperature to 160°C/fan 140°C/gas 3 and continue to cook the meringue for 20–25 minutes, until lightly tinged golden and set.

Dust a sheet of non-stick baking paper with icing sugar. As soon as the meringue is ready, turn it out on to the icing sugar and leave to cool.

For the filling, peel, deseed and slice the papaya, then toss with the lemon juice. In a bowl, whisk together the yoghurt and icing sugar and chill. Warm the marmalade slightly (this will make it easier to spread), chopping any large pieces of peel.

To finish, carefully peel away the base paper from the meringue and spread with the barely warm grapefruit marmalade. Leave to cool. Next, spread the yoghurt mixture on top of the marmalade, then scatter with the papaya. Roll up the roulade, starting from one of the shorter sides. Transfer to a serving plate, dust lightly with icing sugar and sprinkle with the extra grated coconut. Serve straight away.

SAUTERNES CUSTARDS WITH PRUNE COMPOTE

Serves 6

An elegant dessert, based on a French classic. You need to make the custards the day before you want to serve them.

FOR THE CARAMEL
150g caster sugar
2 tablespoons Sauternes, Moscatel or other sweet pudding wine
2 tablespoons thin shred marmalade – I like to use Seville orange marmalade for this recipe

FOR THE CUSTARDS
1 large egg
2 large egg yolks
75g caster sugar
400ml double cream
75ml milk
1 tablespoon Sauternes or other sweet pudding wine

FOR THE PRUNE COMPOTE
100ml Sauternes or other sweet pudding wine
1 tablespoon thin shred marmalade (see above)
100ml freshly squeezed orange juice
200g pitted Agen prunes

For the compote, mix the wine, marmalade and orange juice in a medium pan and heat over a low heat, stirring, to melt the marmalade. Add the prunes, bring to simmering point, then tip into a bowl, cover and set aside.

In a bowl, whisk the egg and yolks with the 75g of sugar. Heat the cream, milk and pudding wine in a medium pan until it just reaches simmering point, then take it off the heat and leave it to cool for 5 minutes before pouring it on to the egg mixture, whisking.

Put six lightly oiled 150ml capacity ramekins (or similarly sized heatproof pots) into a roasting tin or baking dish.

For the caramel, tip the caster sugar into a small pan in an even layer – I use a small frying pan – and heat it over a low flame. Once the sugar starts to liquefy, give it a stir and when it has all melted, leave the caramel to bubble and turn a hazelnut brown. Take the pan off the heat and let it cool for a few minutes.

Meanwhile, in a jug, mix the 2 tablespoons of pudding wine with 75ml of hot water (from a boiled kettle) and the 2 tablespoons of marmalade. Add the contents of the jug, little by little, to the caramel, stirring all the time. Return the pan to a low heat if necessary, to melt any sugary lumps – if you still have the odd one or two it doesn't matter, just leave them in the pan when you put the caramel into the ramekins.

SAUTERNES CUSTARDS WITH PRUNE COMPOTE
Continued

Spoon the caramel into the bottom of the ramekins, dividing it equally, then set aside for 45 minutes or until cooled. (If some caramel has set in the pan, the best way to remove it is to add boiling water and leave it to soak.) Strain the custard through a sieve and into a jug.

Preheat the oven to 150°C/fan 130°C/gas 2. Pour the custard slowly into the ramekins. Add boiling water from the kettle to the roasting tin or baking dish, to come halfway up the ramekins, then bake for 30 minutes. Remove the custards from the oven, leave them to cool in the tin or dish, then remove them and chill overnight.

Take the custards out of the fridge 30 minutes before you want to serve them. Run a small sharp knife around the inside of each one, then tip on to individual plates. Serve with the prunes, spooning a little of the soaking juice over the fruit.

SYLLABUB-TOPPED RHUBARB MARMALADE TRIFLE
Serves 8

Often the first of the early forced Yorkshire rhubarb appears in the shops before Christmas, making this recipe ideal for festive or New Year celebrations. When January arrives, rhubarb is readily available and certainly perks up my appetite for getting back to the kitchen; the shocking pink, palate-awakening spears seem the perfect antidote to the cold grey skies. Start this recipe the day before you want to serve it, so that the jelly has time to set overnight.

400g rhubarb
75g golden caster sugar
zest of 1 orange
a small handful of skin-on almonds (about 25g)
2 leaves (4g) of fine leaf gelatine
250ml freshly squeezed orange juice
100ml Prosecco (or Cava)
8 trifle sponges
5 tablespoons Seville orange marmalade
300ml custard, ready-made or homemade, chilled

FOR THE SYLLABUB
75g golden caster sugar
50ml Prosecco (or Cava)
juice of 1 lemon
300ml whipping cream

SYLLABUB-TOPPED RHUBARB MARMALADE TRIFLE
Continued

Preheat the oven to 180°C/fan 160°C/gas 4. Cut the rhubarb into bite-size pieces. Scatter in a shallow ovenproof dish with the sugar and orange zest. Bake uncovered for 20–25 minutes, until the rhubarb is soft but still holding shape. Leave to cool. Scatter the almonds on a small baking tray and bake at the same time as the rhubarb, for 8–10 minutes, till toasted, then cool.

Soak the gelatine leaves in a shallow bowl of cold water for 10 minutes. Bring the orange juice and Prosecco to simmering point over a gentle heat, then leave to cool for 5 minutes. Squeeze the excess water out of the gelatine leaves and stir them into the warm juice, to dissolve. Tip this jelly mixture into a bowl, leave to cool for an hour.

Spread one side of each trifle sponge with 1 teaspoon of marmalade, halve the sponges and arrange them in a trifle bowl. Strain the cold rhubarb (stir the juice into the jelly mixture) and spoon on top of the sponges. Pour the jelly mixture on top. Cover and chill overnight. For the syllabub, mix the sugar, Prosecco and lemon juice in a bowl, cover and set aside overnight.

To finish, mix the custard with the remaining marmalade and spoon it over the jelly. Softly whip the cream, then gradually whisk in the lemon mix until the cream forms peaks. Top the trifle and chill for up to an hour. Sliver the almonds and sprinkle on top.

CLEMENTINE CHRISTMAS PUDDING

Serves 12

Christmas pudding should be juicy and full of fruitfulness; this festive offering has a whole clementine in the centre to impart citrus flavour and moisture as the pudding bubbles and steams.

---

1 small Bramley cooking apple (about 200g)

1 small carrot

100g skin-on almonds

150g fresh white breadcrumbs

200g vegetarian suet

300g light muscovado sugar

100g dark muscovado sugar

1 tablespoon freshly grated nutmeg

2 teaspoons ground cinnamon

175g plain flour

150g sultanas

150g raisins

100g chopped pitted prunes

4 large eggs

3 tablespoons of your favourite marmalade

2 tablespoons Cointreau

zest and juice of 3 clementines, plus 1 small whole clementine

soft butter, for greasing

Continued

CLEMENTINE CHRISTMAS PUDDING
Continued

FOR THE CANDIED CLEMENTINE SLICES
50g caster sugar
1 clementine, sliced

FOR THE CLEMENTINE CREAM
300ml whipping cream, chilled
1 tablespoon icing sugar
zest of 2 clementines
1 tablespoon marmalade
1–2 teaspoons Cointreau (if you like)

Peel, core and grate the apple, peel and grate the carrot and chop the almonds. Put all three ingredients into a very large mixing bowl with the breadcrumbs, suet, sugars, spices, flour and dried fruit, and stir to mix.

In a small bowl, whisk the eggs with the marmalade, Cointreau and clementine zest and juice, then pour into the dry ingredients. Stir everything thoroughly together.

Pile a third of the mixture into a buttered 1.5 litre pudding basin (I use a stoneware one). Nestle the whole clementine in the middle, then tightly pack the rest of the mixture around and on top of it.

Cut out a large square of non-stick baking paper and butter one side of it. Cut out a square of kitchen foil, the same size, and place both on top of the basin, with the buttered side of the baking paper face down first. Make a pleat in the middle of the paper and foil, folding them together – this will give room for the pudding to expand as it cooks. Tightly secure the foil and paper with a double-length string around the top of the basin (you will need the help of another pair of hands to do this), then cross the string over the top and secure it on the other side – this makes a handle for you to use to lift the hot pudding out of the pan once it is cooked.

Steam the pudding for 4 hours – I use a large pan with a fan steamer (or saucer) in the bottom. Make sure the water stays at a steady but gentle boil, and when you need to top it up, do so from a boiling kettle.

Leave the cooked pudding to cool. Once cold, remove the paper and foil and replace with a fresh set, then store the pudding in a cool, dry place until Christmas Day, when it will need a further 2 hours' steaming.

For the candied clementine slices – which can be made a day or two ahead – dissolve the 50g sugar in 50ml water in a small pan over a gentle heat, stirring to make sure the sugar doesn't stick. Simmer the clementine slices, in the syrup, uncovered in a single layer for 30 minutes, turning halfway. Transfer the slices to non-stick baking paper to cool.

CLEMENTINE CHRISTMAS PUDDING
Continued

For the clementine cream, whip the chilled cream with the icing sugar, then fold in the zest, marmalade and a little Cointreau, if using. Serve with the pudding, topped with the candied clementine slices, with pride.

SEVILLE ORANGE POSSET
Serves 4–6

A posset is a lightly set cream, in which the juice acts as the setting agent. Serve it in tiny glasses – a few mouthfuls is just enough, as it's luxuriously velvety and rich.

300ml double cream
100g golden caster sugar
50g runny honey (I use orange blossom honey)
juice of 3–5 bitter Seville oranges (you need 125ml juice)
4–6 teaspoons of your favourite marmalade – try Seville
    orange, quince and sweet orange, tangerine, lemon and
    lime, or lime and grapefruit
small dainty biscuits, to serve

Put the cream, sugar and honey into a medium pan and stir over a low heat for a couple of minutes, until the sugar dissolves. Now bring to the boil and boil for 3 minutes exactly, giving it a stir now and then.

Turn off the heat and leave the cream to settle for 5 minutes, then stir in the Seville orange juice. Leave to cool slightly.

Put a teaspoon of marmalade into each of six tiny glasses, top up with the posset mixture and cover and chill until softly set, ideally overnight. Serve lightly chilled, with a small, dainty biscuit on the side.

SEVILLE ORANGE POSSET
Continued

ALSO TRY ...

Bergamot posset – make as above, using bergamot juice instead
of Seville orange juice. Depending on the size of the fruit you will
need 2–3 bergamots for 125ml of juice. Use lemon or, even
better, lemon and bergamot marmalade in each glass.

GALVINS' RUM BABAS WITH MARMALADE AND RAISINS

Serves 10

This recipe is based on one I use from *Galvin: A Cookbook de Luxe*, written by Chris and Jeff Galvin, chef brothers extraordinaire. I have eaten rum babas at the Galvins' restaurants and they are so good. Here is their classic version with my marmalade twist.

75g golden raisins (or sultanas)

125g unsalted butter, plus a little extra for greasing

65ml whole milk

2 medium eggs

250g strong plain white flour, plus a little extra for dusting

3g sea salt

10g golden caster sugar

1 x 7g sachet of fast-action dried yeast

50ml dark rum

FOR THE MARMALADE AND RAISIN SYRUP

600g golden caster sugar

500ml dark rum

200g large golden raisins (or sultanas)

3 tablespoons Seville orange marmalade (the ginger and rum variety is particularly good here)

Continued

GALVINS' RUM BABAS WITH MARMALADE AND RAISINS
Continued

FOR THE CHANTILLY CREAM
200ml chilled whipping cream
2 tablespoons crème fraîche
20g icing sugar
1 vanilla pod, split in half lengthways and seeds scraped out

---

For the dough, put the 75g of raisins into a bowl, cover with boiling water and leave to soak for an hour.

Melt the butter and leave it to cool. Heat the milk and leave that to cool too – both should be lukewarm when you add them to the mixer. Drain the raisins and lightly beat the eggs in a cup.

Tip the flour into the bowl of a free-standing mixer fitted with a dough hook. Add the salt, caster sugar and yeast and stir together. Turn the mixer on to a medium speed, add the milk and eggs and mix until the dough comes together. Now, slowly add the melted butter and mix until it has been incorporated. Finally, mix in the soaked raisins.

Transfer the dough to a clean mixing bowl (don't wash the mixer bowl and dough hook, as you will be using them again), cover it with cling film and leave at room temperature until the dough has doubled in size. I pop the bowl into the warming drawer of my oven set on the lowest heat and the dough takes around an hour to rise.

Lightly butter 10 holes of a muffin tin and dust each one with flour – to do this, add a little flour to each hole, tip the tin from side to side so the flour more or less coats the sides of each hole, then tip out the excess.

Return the risen dough to the mixer and mix on a high speed for 2 minutes, to knock the air out. Spoon the dough into the holes of the muffin tin, dividing it equally – it will come about halfway up each one. Cover the tin loosely with cling film and leave in a warm place again until the dough is doubled in size and has reached the top of the holes (about 30–45 minutes). Preheat the oven to 220°C/fan 200°C/gas 7.

Bake the babas for 5 minutes, then reduce the oven temperature to 200°C/fan 180°C/gas 6 and cook them for 12–15 minutes longer, until golden. Remove from the oven, turn out on to a wire rack and leave to cool.

For the syrup, put the caster sugar and the 500ml of rum into a wide-bottomed pan with 1 litre of water and slowly bring to the boil, stirring occasionally to dissolve the sugar. Put the 200g of raisins into a smallish bowl. Remove the syrup from the heat and add enough syrup to the raisins to just cover them. Chop the marmalade, then stir it into the syrup and raisins and leave to cool.

Put half the baked babas into the rest of the hot syrup, leaving them for 10–15 minutes to absorb syrup until they swell and are

GALVINS' RUM BABAS WITH MARMALADE AND RAISINS
Continued

---

completely moist throughout; turn them over halfway. Repeat with the rest of the babas and syrup. Use a fish slice or slotted spoon to carefully remove the soaked babas to a wire rack set over a baking tray so they can drain. Drizzle the 50ml rum evenly over the babas, allowing it to soak in.

For the Chantilly cream, whip all the ingredients together. Serve the rum babas with a spoonful or two of the marmalade and raisin syrup and a spoonful of cream.

BLOOD ORANGE GRANITA

Serves 8–10

This granita is also delicious made with pink grapefruit marmalade and pink grapefruit juice.

4 or 5 sprigs of rosemary
100g caster sugar
3 tablespoons blood orange and vanilla marmalade
200ml freshly squeezed blood orange juice (from 3–4 fruit)
juice of 2 lemons

Lightly bruise the rosemary by gently tapping the stalks and leaves with a knife or the end of a rolling pin. Put the sprigs into a pan with the sugar and 600ml of water. Heat gently, stirring now and then, until the sugar has dissolved, then leave to cool.

Chop the marmalade and mix it with the orange juice, lemon juice and cooled syrup – you can discard the rosemary now, as it has done its work.

Pour the liquid into a shallow plastic container and freeze for 4–5 hours, until the edges are beginning to crystallise. Fork the mix, freeze it for a further 4–5 hours until it is soft-frozen, then fork it again so that the texture of the granita is like slushy snow. Return it to the freezer until you want to serve it. To serve, spoon into small glasses and eat with teaspoons.

BLOOD ORANGE GRANITA
Continued

ALSO TRY ...

Blood orange and Campari granita – leave out the rosemary and add 75ml of Campari; mix it with the marmalade, juices and cooled syrup.

PRUNE, ORANGE AND ARMAGNAC BREAD AND BUTTER PUDDING

Serves 6–8

It's such a shame that lots of people have been put off bread and butter pudding by stodgy lacklustre recipes. This, I promise, is in a different league – boozy custard, juicy prunes and buttery brioche. Eat warm, with chilled cream.

200g brioche – use Seville orange brioche (page 78) if you have made one

about 30g very soft butter, for spreading

2 tablespoons marmalade, Seville orange or sweet orange, plus extra for brushing

125g pitted prunes

50g walnut pieces

FOR THE CUSTARD

300ml milk

150ml double cream

1 vanilla pod

3 large eggs

50g caster sugar

1 tablespoon Armagnac (or whisky)

2 tablespoons marmalade (see above)

PRUNE, ORANGE AND ARMAGNAC BREAD AND BUTTER PUDDING
Continued

For the custard, pour the milk and cream into a pan. Split the vanilla pod in half lengthways, scrape out the seeds and add these and the pod to the pan. Stir, bring to simmering point, then turn off the heat and leave to cool.

In a bowl, whisk together the eggs, sugar, Armagnac, marmalade and the cold vanilla-infused milk and cream (you can discard the vanilla pod now).

Slice the brioche and spread one side of each with butter and marmalade. Chop the prunes. Layer the brioche slices with the prunes and walnuts in a buttered 20cm ovenproof dish 4cm deep. Pour over the custard and gently press the slices down so that as many as possible are immersed in the custard. Leave the pudding to stand for 30 minutes – this gives the brioche a chance to absorb the custard. Preheat the oven to 160°C/fan 140°C/gas 3.

Bake the pudding for 1 hour to 1 hour 15 minutes, or until puffed up and set in the middle. Warm a little extra marmalade and brush over the top of the pudding. Leave it to cool for 20 minutes or so before eating.

TEATIME

CHOCOLATE, APRICOT AND MARMALADE MUFFINS
Serves 12

You can never have too many muffin recipes. Eat these while they are still warm.

100g dark chocolate (around 70% cocoa solids)

100g ready-to-eat dried apricots

150g butter

4 large eggs

100g light or dark muscovado sugar

150ml milk

100ml double cream

5 tablespoons Seville orange marmalade

200g self-raising flour

2 teaspoons baking powder

Preheat the oven to 200°C/fan 180°C/gas 6 and line a 12-hole muffin tin with muffin cases. Chop the chocolate and the apricots into small pieces. Melt the butter in a small pan.

In a large bowl, whisk together the eggs, sugar, milk, cream, 2 tablespoons of the marmalade and the melted butter. Sift the flour and baking powder into the bowl and add a generous pinch of salt. Add the chopped chocolate and apricots and gently fold everything together. Don't over-mix.

CHOCOLATE, APRICOT AND MARMALADE MUFFINS
Continued

Spoon the mixture into the muffin cases – the mixture will be wet but that is how it should be. Bake the muffins for 25 minutes. Towards the end of the cooking time, heat the remaining 3 tablespoons of marmalade in a small pan with a teaspoon of water.

When ready, take the muffins out of the oven and spoon a little of the melted marmalade on top of each one.

MARMALADE, DATE AND PEAR MUFFIN CAKE WITH NUTMEG CRUMBLE
Serves 16

Best eaten on the day it is made – a bake with an oaty crumble topping which is spiced with nutmeg and adds crunch. I can't resist anything with crumble on or in it, and often use a crumble mix to top cakes and muffins.

150g butter
2 ripe medium bananas
2 ripe but firm pears
150g pitted Medjool dates
3 tablespoons of your favourite marmalade
zest of 1 orange
175ml double cream
100g golden caster sugar
2 large eggs
250g self-raising flour
1 rounded teaspoon baking powder
1 teaspoon freshly grated nutmeg
a pinch of ground cloves

FOR THE CRUMBLE TOPPING
40g chilled butter, in small pieces
50g self-raising flour
40g demerara sugar
25g porridge oats
1 teaspoon freshly grated nutmeg

MARMALADE, DATE AND PEAR MUFFIN CAKE WITH NUTMEG CRUMBLE
Continued

Preheat the oven to 200°C/fan 180°C/gas 6. Melt the 150g of butter and leave to cool slightly. Peel and mash the bananas. Core the pears and chop into bite-size pieces (no need to peel them) and chop the dates too.

In a bowl, whisk together the marmalade, zest, cream, sugar, eggs and the melted butter.

To make the crumble topping, rub the butter into the flour until it resembles breadcrumbs, then mix in the sugar, oats and nutmeg.

Tip the 250g of flour into a large bowl with the baking powder and a pinch of salt, and add the nutmeg, cloves, banana, pear and the cream mixture. Fold together to combine – don't over-mix.

Spoon three-quarters of the mixture into a lightly buttered 23–24cm springform tin. Scatter the dates on top, then add the rest of the mixture, followed by the crumble topping. Bake the cake for 1 hour, until risen and set in the middle. Check it after 45 minutes and if the top is browning too much, cover it with foil. Leave to cool in the tin.

MARMALADE, PLUM AND HAZELNUT CAKE
Serves 12

This cake is as simple as pie to make, and is as good with a cuppa as it is as a dessert, with some Greek yoghurt or ice cream on the side.

50g soft unsalted butter
50g golden caster sugar
1 tablespoon of your favourite marmalade
6 plums

FOR THE CAKE
100g hazelnuts
175g soft unsalted butter
125g golden caster sugar
50g light or dark muscovado sugar
2 teaspoons ground mixed spice
3 large eggs
2 tablespoons marmalade (see above)
100g plain flour
2 teaspoons baking powder
100g polenta

MARMALADE, PLUM AND HAZELNUT CAKE
Continued

Preheat the oven to 180°C/fan 160°C/gas 4. In a small bowl and using a wooden spoon, mix the 50g of butter and 50g of sugar together until smooth, then chop the tablespoon of marmalade in a cup using scissors and stir that in too. Spread this mixture over the base of a buttered and base-lined 20cm springform tin.

Next, halve and de-stone the plums and place them on the sugary butter, cut side downwards – this will be the top of your cake once it is baked.

Whiz the hazelnuts in a food processor until ground. Then mix with all the rest of the cake ingredients and a pinch of salt – use a mixing bowl and an electric hand mixer or a free-standing mixer. Once thoroughly combined, spoon the cake mixture on top of the plums and smooth the top with a knife.

Put the tin on a baking tray and bake the cake for 1 hour 25 minutes to 1 hour 30 minutes, loosely covering the top with foil after about 45 minutes to prevent it from over-browning.

Leave the cake to cool in the tin before releasing it and inverting it on to a flat plate or board.

JAFFA BROWNIES
Makes 16

Marmalade adds extra gooey-ness to these soft and squidgy dark chocolate brownies.

150g dark chocolate (around 70% cocoa solids)
150g really soft butter, plus extra for greasing
300g dark muscovado sugar
3 large eggs
3 tablespoons Seville orange marmalade
1 teaspoon pure or natural orange extract
zest of 1 large orange
25g cocoa powder
135g plain flour
1 teaspoon ground cinnamon

Preheat the oven to 180°C/fan 160°C/gas 4. Break the chocolate into pieces, then melt it in a bowl over a pan of barely simmering water and leave it to cool slightly.

Using an electric hand whisk, whisk the butter and sugar together in a mixing bowl for a few minutes to combine and become creamy. Lightly beat the eggs with the marmalade, orange extract and orange zest in a small bowl, then gradually add them to the butter mixture, mixing all the time.

JAFFA BROWNIES
Continued

Sift in the cocoa, flour and cinnamon, then add the cooled melted chocolate and a pinch of salt and mix to combine.

Tip the mixture into a lightly buttered 18cm square tin, base-lined with non-stick baking paper. Bake the brownies for 35–40 minutes or until just set in the middle, leave them to cool in the tin, then cut into squares.

MARMALADE AND SOUR CHERRY FLAPJACKS
Makes 8

Vary the seeds according to what you have in the cupboard. Use regular porridge oats in the mix rather than the jumbo variety, otherwise it will be trickier to cut the flapjacks into bars.

150g butter, plus extra for greasing
50g demerara sugar
3 tablespoons of your favourite marmalade
1 tablespoon golden syrup
100g dried cherries (or cranberries)
225g porridge oats
2 tablespoons mixed seeds, such as sunflower, pumpkin and linseed

Preheat the oven to 180°C/fan 160°C/gas 4. In a medium pan, melt the butter with the sugar, marmalade and golden syrup, stirring. Meanwhile, roughly chop the cherries and put them into a mixing bowl with the oats and seeds.

Pour the melted butter mixture into the bowl and stir to thoroughly combine. Tip the flapjack mixture into a lightly greased 20cm square tin – a tin with a removable base is ideal, as it makes it easy to get the flapjacks out. Press the mixture down into the tin to smooth the top. Bake the flapjacks for 35–40 minutes, or until lightly golden.

MARMALADE AND SOUR CHERRY FLAPJACKS
Continued

Leave to cool in the tin for 15–20 minutes, then mark into 8 bars with a knife and loosen around the edges. Leave the flapjack bars to cool completely before removing from the tin.

QUINCE BAKEWELL TARTS
Makes 24

Fit enough to grace any elegant tea-time table, you can of course make these with any marmalade. However, the quince is particularly good.

500g shortcrust or sweet shortcrust pastry
2 large eggs
100g soft butter
75g golden caster sugar
100g ground almonds
25g plain flour, plus extra for rolling out
½ teaspoon almond extract
about 8 tablespoons quince and sweet orange marmalade, or
    another favourite
icing sugar, for dusting

On a lightly floured surface, roll out half the pastry until it is about 3mm thick. Using an 8–9cm fluted cutter, stamp out 12 rounds and use to line the holes of a 12-hole shallow bun or patty tin. Repeat with the rest of the pastry and another tin. Chill the pastry-lined tins for 30 minutes.

Preheat the oven to 200°C/fan 180°C/gas 6 and make the filling. Lightly beat the eggs in a small bowl with a fork, then whiz them in a food processor with the soft butter, caster sugar, ground almonds, flour, almond extract and a pinch of salt until combined.

QUINCE BAKEWELL TARTS
Continued

Add a generous teaspoonful of marmalade to each pastry cup, then spoon the filling on top of the marmalade, smoothing it out with the back of a teaspoon.

Bake the tarts for 15 minutes, until risen and golden. Cool on a wire rack, then lightly dust with icing sugar.

STICKY GINGER AND MARMALADE PARKIN
Makes 16 squares

Being married to a Yorkshireman, parkin – a type of ginger cake originating in the north of England – is a favourite in our house. Marmalade adds richness and stickiness, and the parkin keeps really well, in fact it improves with time.

175g plain flour
75g golden caster sugar
100g light muscovado sugar
125g porridge oats, plus extra for sprinkling
3 teaspoons ground ginger
a generous grating of nutmeg
1 teaspoon bicarbonate of soda
100g butter
200ml milk
3 tablespoons black treacle
3 tablespoons Seville orange, dark and moody, four fruit or
    apple harvest marmalade

Preheat the oven to 150°C/fan 130°C/gas 2. Sift the flour into a large bowl, then mix in the sugars, oats, ground ginger, nutmeg, bicarbonate of soda and a couple of pinches of salt.

STICKY GINGER AND MARMALADE PARKIN
Continued

Cut the butter into pieces and put them into a small pan with the milk, treacle and marmalade. Heat until the butter has melted, then give everything a stir and, using a balloon whisk, mix the warm liquid into the dry ingredients.

Pour the mixture into a lightly buttered and base-lined 20cm square tin (don't use a loose-bottomed tin, the mixture is too runny). Sprinkle the top of the parkin with extra oats. Bake it for 45 minutes, or until risen and set in the middle. Leave to cool in the tin, then cut into 16 squares.

CHOCOLATE MARMALADE MINI MADELEINES

Makes about 40 (or 12 regular madeleines)

A mini madeleine mould is a new discovery for me – it's one of those bendy, silicone type moulds and I use it all the time. Bite-size chocolatey nutty madeleines now tempt me from the cookie jar in the kitchen; they are a good size to serve with ice cream or coffee – small and perfectly formed. If you want to make regular-size madeleines, bake them for 10–12 minutes in a 12-hole madeleine tin.

25g blanched hazelnuts

2 tablespoons marmalade (I like to use Seville orange for this recipe)

50g dark chocolate (around 70% cocoa solids)

40g unsalted butter, plus extra for greasing

25g self-raising flour

¼ teaspoon baking powder

1 medium egg

50g light muscovado sugar

Preheat the oven to 200°C/fan 180°C/gas 6. Scatter the hazelnuts on a baking tray and bake for 6–7 minutes, until golden, then leave to cool.

CHOCOLATE MARMALADE MINI MADELEINES
Continued

Put the marmalade into a small heatproof bowl and finely chop any large shreds of peel with scissors. Chop the chocolate, cut the butter into small pieces, and add those to the bowl too. Put the bowl over a pan of barely simmering water. Leave to gently melt, stirring now and then. When ready, take the bowl off the heat. Meanwhile, whiz the hazelnuts in a blender until finely chopped and sift the flour into a bowl with the baking powder and a pinch of salt.

Next, using an electric hand whisk, whisk the egg and sugar together in another bowl till they are mousse-like in texture; this will take about 5 minutes.

Add half the chocolate mixture, half the nuts and half the flour to the beaten egg, folding them in gently. Add the rest of the ingredients and fold in again.

Fill a greased 24-hole mini madeleine mould – put it on a tray first to steady it – with the mixture and bake the madeleines for 8–10 minutes. Cool them briefly in the mould before turning them out on to a wire rack and baking the next batch.

A Pot of Marmalade

CARDAMOM, PISTACHIO AND MARMALADE DRIZZLE LOAF

Serves 10–12

We ate far too much of this moist, crumbly loaf, with its Middle Eastern flavours, while I was recipe testing for this book. It slices well, so it's a good cake to transport to picnics or for weekends away.

seeds from 8 cardamom pods
200g shelled pistachios
150g soft butter, in pieces, plus extra for greasing
125g golden caster sugar
3 large eggs
100g self-raising flour
1 teaspoon baking powder
2 tablespoons of your favourite marmalade
2 teaspoons orange blossom water

FOR THE DRIZZLE
3 tablespoons marmalade (see above)
juice of 1 lemon
50g caster sugar
1 teaspoon orange flower water

Preheat the oven to 170°C/fan 150°C/gas 3 and prepare a 19 × 9 × 7cm loaf tin – butter the inside and line the base with non-stick baking paper, or use a non-stick loaf liner.

CARDAMOM, PISTACHIO AND MARMALADE DRIZZLE LOAF
Continued

Crush the cardamom seeds in a pestle and mortar. Whiz half the pistachios in a processor or blender until very finely chopped.

Using an electric hand whisk, beat together the butter, sugar, eggs, flour, baking powder, marmalade, orange blossom water, crushed cardamom seeds, chopped pistachios and a pinch of salt in a bowl until combined. Roughly chop the rest of the pistachios and stir them into the cake mix.

Tip the mixture into the prepared tin and bake for 1 hour to 1 hour 15 minutes, covering the top of the loaf with foil halfway through to prevent it over-browning.

For the drizzle, gently heat the marmalade, then combine with the other ingredients in a bowl and spoon on top of the warm loaf. Leave to cool in the tin, and serve cut in slices.

MINI FAT RASCALS
Makes 16

Fat rascals, a cross between a scone and a cake, are one of the
most popular cakes at the famous Bettys Tea Rooms in Yorkshire,
where the recipe is a fiercely guarded secret. This mini version,
inspired by a family friend, is, I think, a good competitor. The
rascals freeze well if you don't want to eat them all on the same
day.

150g plain flour
150g self-raising flour
1 teaspoon baking powder
150g cold butter
100g pitted prunes (or dates)
100g dark chocolate (around 70% cocoa solids)
2 medium eggs
2 tablespoons Seville orange, dark and moody, four fruit or
    apple harvest marmalade
75g caster sugar
½ teaspoon freshly grated nutmeg

TO GLAZE AND FINISH
1 medium egg yolk
8 blanched almonds
2 tablespoons marmalade (see above)

MINI FAT RASCALS
Continued

Preheat the oven to 200°C/fan 180°C/gas 6. Sieve the flours and baking powder into a large mixing bowl and stir to mix.

Cube the butter, then rub it into the flour – you can do this by hand or in a food processor. Chop the prunes and chocolate into smallish pieces. Lightly beat the eggs with the marmalade in a cup, chopping any large pieces of peel with scissors. Add the sugar, nutmeg and eggs to the dough and mix, then finally mix in the prunes and chocolate – if you are using a food processor, only briefly mix the dough when you add these last two ingredients, as you still want them to be in small chunks.

Divide the dough into 16 pieces and roll them into balls. Place the balls on two large greased baking sheets and flatten them very slightly with your palm.

In a small bowl, lightly beat the egg yolk with a pinch of salt and a few drops of water, and brush on top of the fat rascals. Halve the almonds and push one half into the top of each rascal.

Bake the fat rascals for 15–20 minutes, or until lightly golden. Transfer them to a rack to cool. Warm the 2 tablespoons of marmalade – chopping any large pieces of peel – and brush the marmalade on top of the fat rascals.

HONEY & CO ZESTY MARMALADE-FILLED COOKIES

Serves 7

One of my favourite new discoveries is Honey & Co, a pocket-sized Middle Eastern restaurant in London. By day, locals pass by to pick up coffee and one of Sarit's drool-worthy cakes or cookies, and by night she and her husband Itamar turn the 10-table space into a buzzing restaurant. Sarit wrote this recipe for me, which is a dream come true – a little flavour of Honey & Co in my own book. The semolina gives the cookie dough a great texture and a crispy outside, the perfect contrast to the marmalade inside.

100g plain flour, plus extra for rolling out

70g semolina

zest of ½ a lemon and ½ tablespoon lemon juice

zest of 1 clementine and ½ tablespoon clementine juice

125g soft butter, cut in pieces

25g icing sugar, plus a little extra for dusting

7 teaspoons of your favourite marmalade

Put the 100g of flour, the semolina and the lemon and clementine zests into a bowl and mix together. Using a table knife, cut the soft butter into the mixed flour until it is in large blended clumps, then mix in the icing sugar using the knife.

HONEY & CO ZESTY MARMALADE-FILLED COOKIES
Continued

Combine the lemon and clementine juices in a cup. Sprinkle the juice over the flour mix and incorporate them into the dough. The dough will be quite sticky.

Cover the dough with cling film and allow it to rest for half an hour in a cool place, but don't refrigerate it – this time will allow the semolina to expand and the resulting dough will have a melt-in-the-mouth texture. Preheat your oven to 190°C/fan 170°C/gas 5.

On a floured surface, roll out the dough to a thickness of about 5mm and use a 7cm round cutter or a wine glass with a similar diameter to stamp out 2 rounds. Place one round in the palm of your hand and spoon a teaspoon of marmalade in the middle. Take the other round, place on top, and gently squeeze the sides together to incorporate the filling. Place the filled cookies on a lined baking tray. Repeat with the rest of the dough to make 7 assembled cookies.

Bake the cookies in the centre of the oven for 12–15 minutes, or until the pastry is lightly golden. Allow them to cool for 10 minutes on the baking tray before transferring them to a wire rack to complete cooling. You can dust them with a little icing sugar before eating if you like, and they will keep well in an airtight box for 2 days.

FIGGY PUDDING CHRISTMAS CAKE
Serves at least 20

Make this cake up to six weeks before Christmas and store it,
wrapped, in an airtight box. Christmas cake freezes well too, but
there seems little point when you can store it and feed it with a
little extra booze as Christmas creeps closer. If you are also
making mincemeat, a tablespoon of marmalade adds an extra
citrusy edge.

150g dried figs
225g sultanas
150g currants
225g raisins
150ml Pedro Ximénez sherry, plus extra for feeding
5 large eggs
275g soft butter
150g light muscovado sugar
100g molasses sugar
grated zest and juice of 1 lemon
2 tablespoons black treacle
3 tablespoons Seville orange, dark and moody or four fruit
    marmalade
350g self-raising flour
3 teaspoons ground mixed spice
200g undyed glacé cherries
100g unblanched almonds
50g crystallised ginger pieces (or chopped crystallised ginger)
100g walnut pieces (or chopped pecans)

FIGGY PUDDING CHRISTMAS CAKE
Continued

Chop the dried figs into small pieces, discarding their stubby stalks.
Put into a bowl with the sultanas, currants, raisins and Pedro
Ximénez sherry, stir together and set aside for a few hours (or
cover and leave overnight).

Preheat the oven to 150°C/fan 130°C/gas 2. Crack the eggs into a
small bowl and beat lightly with a fork. In a free-standing mixer or
using a large mixing bowl and an electric whisk, beat together the
butter and sugars for about 5 minutes. Add the eggs, little by little,
then the lemon zest and juice, treacle and marmalade. Now sift in
the flour and spice and mix together.

Halve the cherries and roughly chop the almonds. Stir both into
the mixture along with the soaked dried fruit (and any sherry left
in the bowl), the ginger, walnut pieces and a generous pinch of
salt. Mix everything together thoroughly, then spoon the cake
mixture into a buttered and lined (base and sides) 20cm square
cake tin. I use a loose-bottomed tin.

Bake the cake for 2 hours 30 minutes, or until a skewer gently inserted into the middle comes out without cake mixture on it, covering the top of the cake with foil if it is over-browning towards the end of the cooking time. Cool the cake in the tin, then take it out and wrap it in several layers of cling film and kitchen foil before putting it into a large airtight box. Store until Christmas – it will keep for 6 weeks. Feed the cake from time to time with a little sherry by making small insertions all over the top and drizzling a little more PX sherry over the holes with a teaspoon.

To decorate, warm the marmalade, then sieve it and brush some of it over the surface of the cake. Top the cake with a mixture of whole nuts and dried fruits and brush them with more of the warm marmalade as a glaze – it helps the topping to stay on the cake. You may need to add a little boiling water to the glaze for it to be a suitable consistency to brush. Leave the cake topping to set before adding a fancy ribbon to tie around the waist of the cake.

MARMALADE, APPLE
AND CLOVE SCONES
Makes 9

These are large square-ish scones rather than the usual round
shape – rustic but light and fluffy-textured.

---

1 tart eating apple or a small Bramley apple (about 175g)

1 large egg

175ml milk, plus extra for brushing

3 tablespoons of your favourite marmalade

450g plain flour, plus extra for dusting

2 teaspoons baking powder

1 tablespoon demerara sugar, plus extra for sprinkling

¼ teaspoon ground cloves

100g soft butter

extra butter and marmalade, to serve

Preheat the oven to 230°C/fan 210°C/gas 8. Peel, core and grate
or finely chop the apple. Lightly beat the egg and milk together in
a small bowl, then stir in the marmalade – use scissors to chop
any large pieces of peel.

Sift the flour and baking powder into a large mixing bowl and stir
in the tablespoon of demerara sugar, the cloves and a pinch of
salt.

Cut the butter into small pieces and scatter over the flour. Using a table knife, cut the fat into the flour, then rub it in using the tips of your fingers – it should resemble breadcrumbs. Add the apple (it doesn't matter if it has slightly discoloured by now) and mix it in.

Now add the egg mixture and cut this into the mix with the knife. Bring the dough together with your hands and turn it out on to a lightly floured surface. Gently pat the dough into a 2cm thick square, then, using a sharp knife, cut this into 9 smaller squares (it doesn't matter if they have slightly triangular rather than 'corner' edges).

Transfer the scones to a large, greased and lightly floured baking tray – I find a fish slice helps – and brush the tops with milk. Lightly dust the scones with flour and sprinkle them with demerara sugar.

Bake the scones for 15–20 minutes, or until risen and lightly golden. Transfer to a cooling rack. Serve warm, split and topped with butter and marmalade.

DRINKS
&
COCKTAILS

MARMALADE FIZZ
Serves 8

A versatile fizz; refreshing in the summer and just the thing for festive parties later in the year. You can prepare the marmalade base and keep it chilled in the fridge until you are ready to pop open the bottle.

---

12 tablespoons marmalade – I like to use Seville orange, tangerine, lemon and lime or quince and sweet orange
200ml Cointreau, chilled
1 bottle of Cava, Prosecco or Champagne, chilled
6 pared pieces of orange peel

First measure the marmalade into the small bowl of a food processor or a liquidiser. Add the chilled Cointreau and whiz together for a minute or so, then strain through a mini-sieve into a measuring jug.

Pour about 2 tablespoons of the boozy marmalade mix into six glasses. Half fill them with chilled fizz, stir, then top up with more.

Squeeze a piece of pared orange peel over each glass to release the essential oils before dropping it into the glass. Serve.

JAMIE OLIVER'S PADDINGTON'S DEMISE
Serves 2

I tried this jam-jar cocktail at a party for the re-launch of Jamie Oliver's restaurant, Fifteen, in east London, and here it is to share with you. At Fifteen they use marmalade vodka, which is delicious, but regular vodka works well too and is easier to buy.

100ml vodka
1 large egg white
2 tablespoons Seville orange marmalade
juice of 1 lemon
2 tablespoons gomme (sugar) syrup
6 dashes of Angostura bitters
4 dashes of orange bitters or orange extract
a few cubes of ice
2 twists of orange peel or slices of orange

Shake the first seven ingredients in a cocktail shaker, add ice, then give everything a second hard shake.

Strain the cocktail into two jam-jars (or glasses), add a couple of cubes of ice to each one and finish with a twist of peel or an orange slice.

A Pot of Marmalade

GRAPEFRUIT, MINT AND LIME PUNCH
Serves 6

For hot sunny days when the barbecue is lit and the living is easy.

---

1 large lime
3 tablespoons marmalade – lime and grapefruit; lemon; or pink
   grapefruit
3 tablespoons gomme (sugar) syrup
500ml pink grapefruit juice, chilled
100ml white rum, chilled
500ml soda water, chilled
a handful of small fresh mint leaves
a generous handful of ice

Cut the lime into 8 wedges and chop the marmalade in a cup,
using scissors, so there are no large pieces of peel.

Put the lime wedges into a large jug, squeezing them as you do so
to release the juice. Add all the other ingredients, including the ice,
and serve.

MARMALADE MARGUERITE
Serves 2

A variation on a classic martini.

> 70ml gin, chilled
> 30ml Noilly Prat, chilled
> juice of 1 clementine
> 1 tablespoon marmalade – Seville orange; tangerine, lemon
>   and lime; or lemon
> a few cubes of ice
> 2 pared pieces of orange peel

Put all the ingredients apart from the ice and orange peel into a cocktail shaker. Shake together.

Add ice and shake again, then pour into two small glasses.

Add a piece of pared orange peel to each one, first squeezing it over the top of the drink to release the aromatic oils.

A TWIST ON A COSMOPOLITAN
Serves 2

Glam and pretty, the quintessential girlie cocktail.

75ml vodka or gin, chilled

25ml Cointreau, chilled

juice of 1 lime

1–2 tablespoons marmalade – Seville orange; tangerine, lemon
   and lime; lime and grapefruit; lemon; or pink grapefruit

75ml chilled cranberry or (white or pink) grapefruit juice (or
   a 50/50 mix)

a few cubes of ice

2 twists of lime peel

Put all the ingredients apart from the ice and lime peel into a
cocktail shaker. Shake together.

Add ice and shake again, then pour into two glasses. Garnish with
a twist of lime.

A MULL FOR A COLD WINTER'S DAY
Serves 4

A change from the usual mulled red wine, this cider mull was inspired by a winter warmer that I sipped on a snowy afternoon while meandering around the food market in Copenhagen. The plump boozy sultanas in the bottom of the drink are a nice surprise.

50g sultanas (or raisins)
75ml dark rum
1 vanilla pod
1 clementine
8–10 cloves
1 eating apple
250ml cloudy apple juice
500ml cider (I use vintage cider)
3 tablespoons marmalade – Seville orange; dark and moody; or four fruit
1 cinnamon stick
a generous grating of nutmeg

FOR THE SPICE BAG
4 cardamom pods
3 allspice berries
a 3cm piece of root ginger
4 black peppercorns

Put the sultanas into a small bowl, add 2 tablespoons of the rum, stir, then set aside to soak.

Now split the vanilla pod in half lengthways and put it into a medium pan. Stud the clementine with the cloves, and core and slice the apple (no need to peel it). Add those to the pan too, with the rest of the rum, the juice, cider, marmalade, cinnamon stick and a grating of nutmeg.

Bash the cardamom pods to split them open, lightly squash the allspice berries, and chop the ginger (no need to peel it). Put these and the peppercorns on to a double-layered square of gauze (or muslin) and gather it together to make a small spice pouch. Put the pouch into the pan. Bring the cider to simmering point, then reduce the heat to low and leave it for 30 minutes; there should barely be a bubble on the surface; give it a stir from time to time.

To serve, remove and discard the spice bag, strain the mulled cider through a sieve, then return it to the pan to gently reheat. Divide the soaked sultanas or raisins among four heatproof glasses or mugs, and top up with the mulled cider.

VIN D'ORANGE
Makes about 2 litres

An adaptation of a Sally Clarke recipe that was introduced to me
by food writer Lucas Hollweg and his partner Lucie. After many
glasses one evening, we decided a marmalade version would be
worth a go, and I have made it several times since. Serve vin
d'orange as a short drink over ice in small glasses with a twist of
orange and lemon, or add soda water for a longer drink and
enjoy it in the shade of the garden on a hot summer's day. It also
makes a delicious base for a Prosecco or Champagne cocktail.
Taste the mix after a couple of weeks and add more sugar if you
think it needs it.

---

2 oranges
½ a lemon
100g marmalade – Seville orange, lemon or pink grapefruit
175g golden caster sugar
1 vanilla pod, split lengthways
1 small cinnamon stick
2 x 750ml bottles of rosé wine – I like to use a Provençal rosé
200ml gin
50ml dark rum

Slice the oranges and the lemon, flicking out the pips as you go.
Put the slices into a large sterilised jar; I use a 2-litre clip-top jar.

Add all the other ingredients apart from the rum. Stir with a long-handled spoon and seal with a tight-fitting lid. Leave the vin d'orange to macerate in a cool place – I usually put it in a garage or cellar – for 6–8 weeks, shaking the jar gently from time to time.

After this time, strain the liquid through a gauze- or muslin-lined sieve set over a large measuring jug or bowl. Stir in the rum, then transfer to sterilised bottles – I chop up the vanilla pod and add a little piece to each bottle, and you can add a small, fresh cinnamon stick too. Store the vin d'orange in a cool place or in the fridge; it keeps well.

WHISKY SOUR
Serves 2

Sip by a roaring fire to warm you from tip to toe.

---

   2 tablespoons marmalade – Seville orange; dark and moody;
      or lemon
   100ml whisky or Bourbon
   juice of 2 lemons
   juice of 2 limes
   1 tablespoon gomme (sugar) syrup

Chop the marmalade in a cup, using scissors, so there are no large pieces of peel, then swirl all the ingredients together in a cocktail shaker or jug. Pour into two glasses.

ACKNOWLEDGEMENTS
&
INDEX

ACKNOWLEDGEMENTS

Well, it's been quite a marmalade adventure and I have treasured every minute of it, with the exception of the February evening when I dropped a large quantity of sticky, warm marmalade on our wooden kitchen floor that ran into every possible nook and cranny and no matter how many times I washed it, the floor still resembled that of a boozer.

Thank you to my agent Heather Holden Brown for holding my hand and to the team at Saltyard: the wonderful and inspiring Elizabeth, Kate (you have won the prize for patience and I owe you many marmalade cakes and cookies) and also to Rosie Gailer, James Edgar and Laura Del Vescovo. Kitchen love goes to Clare, Bren, Vicky and Tamsin for second-testing my recipes and thank you to Jane Hasell-McCosh for welcoming me to the Marmalade Awards, the Gahona family at Ave María Farm for sharing their top quality organic Seville oranges and to José Pizarro, my Spanish mentor, you're a treasure.

This book is for my mum who made me my first slice of home-made marmalade on toast; my dad, whose enthusiasm for everything I do never fails and, above all, for my darling, Matthew, who makes it all worthwhile and, thank goodness, still likes marmalade. xx

INDEX

15-minute lemon passion fruit
   pots 141–2
figgy pudding Christmas cake
   191–3
flapjacks:
   marmalade and sour cherry
      flapjacks 177–8
four fruit marmalade 61–2
G
Galvin's rum babas with
   marmalade and raisins
   159–62
gin:
   Christmas ham with cranber-
      ries and sloe gin 120–2
   lemon and gin marmalade
      52
   a twist on a Cosmopolitan
      203
   vin d'orange 206–7
ginger:
   ginger and rum marmalade
      40
   marmalade, ginger and Seville
      orange ice cream 129–30
   sticky ginger and marmalade
      parkin 181–2

goat's curd:
   bulgar wheat and watercress
      salad with goat's curd
      108–9
granita:
   blood orange granita 163–4
grapefruit:
   coconut, papaya and grape-
      fruit meringue roulade
      146–7
   four fruit marmalade 61–2
   grapefruit, mint and lime
      punch 201
   lime and grapefruit marma-
      lade 56–7
   pink grapefruit marmalade
      63–4
H
ham:
   Christmas ham with cranber-
      ries and sloe gin 120–2
harissa:
   marmalade harissa sausages
      83
hazelnuts:
   marmalade, plum and
      hazelnut cake 173–4

Honey & Co zesty marmalade-filled cookies 189–90
hotcakes:
    apple and marmalade
        hotcakes 86–8

I

ice cream:
    marmalade, ginger and
        Seville orange ice cream
        129–30

J

Jaffa brownies 175–6
jerk-seasoned slow roast
    shoulder of pork with
    pineapple 110–12

K

kumquats:
    kumquat and cranberry
        marmalade 68–9
    roast chicken with perry,
        apples and kumquats
        104–5

L

lamb:
    shoulder of lamb with
        quince and Iranian lime
        114–16

lavender:
    sweet orange and lavender
        marmalade 47
lemons:
    citrus dressing 108–9
    four fruit marmalade
        61–2
    15-minute lemon passion
        fruit pots 141–2
    lemon sunshine marmalade
        50–2
    mini lemon and blackcurrant
        puddings 137–8
    Sicilian lemon marmalade
        54–5
    tangerine, lemon and lime
        marmalade 58–60
limes:
    grapefruit, mint and lime
        punch 201
    lime and grapefruit marmalade 56–7
    shoulder of lamb with
        quince and Iranian lime
        114–16
    tangerine, lemon and lime
        marmalade 58–60